DIOR

STRIP CLUB DIARIES #1

Keisha Floyd

DWE

Dior; Strip Club Diaries #1

© Copyright 2014 by Keisha Floyd

This book is a based on the reflected life and times
of Keisha Floyd. Many names, characters, places and
incident shave been changed to protect others. Any
resemblance to other events, locales or persons in this
book are entirely coincidental.

Acknowledgments:

This book is dedicated to those that embrace me throughout my journey. I am forever grateful for your words of encouragement and guidance.

Keisha Floyd

DIOR

STRIP CLUB
DIARIES #1

Prologue

I looked like a million bucks the night of my first big party. I showed up early on business mode to get everything just right in the back, and it was a packed-ass party as soon as I walked in. Then the DJ called my name from the booth to hit the front stage.

"Dee-orrr! It's your night, baby girl. Everyone give it up for Dior's World Entertainment."

As I approached the front stage to make my grand appearance for the crowd, money started flying from every direction. The DJ continued to yell out my name and tell the people to keep spending their money to make it rain for my birthday. You couldn't even walk on the floor in there without stepping on green dollar bills. As we say in the strip clubs, the green carpet was everywhere. I was even slipping on money as I tried to walk. So the club manager had to call someone to the stage to sweep the money off with a broom.

Once we stacked it all up in big black garbage bags, we counted eight-thousand dollars that night from the dance floor and my performances alone. Then I pulled another five thousand from splitting the door money with Cisco for thirteen thousand dollars.

This is what the fuck I'm talking about! I told myself. That was the kind of money I was trying to make every night. But with thirteen-thousand dollars from just one event, I wouldn't have to grind as hard to get it anymore. Thirteen Gs in one night was real hustling.

I walked backstage, where I had a VIP area set up

for Pinky The Porn Star, who was loud, drinking and having a good time with her manger Danielle and friends. We had porn star Gazelle Triple X in the house too, and a good friend of mine named Patrick. And they were all treating me good on my first big night.

I said, "Hey, y'all," and greeting everyone inside the room, giving Patrick a hug. Patrick was like family to me. I had known him for several years and we had always been nothing but friends.

Cisco had been pretty quiet for most the night, while eyeballing all of the money that I was making in there. But suddenly he wanted to call me over and talk to me from the VIP area.

I walked over to Cisco, smiling and feeling good about our successful night. I asked him, "What's up, babe?" I figured it was something small.

But Cisco goes off on me. "What the fuck you doing hugging up on some nigga?"

Before I could say anything to explain who Patrick was, Cisco swung a punch straight to my stomach and knocked the wind out of me. In pain and shock, I crumpled to the floor and tried to catch my breath. I couldn't believe that he had punched me in my stomach at my big party in front of all of those people. I mean, it was a huge crowd.

You could hear the silence in the room as the people watched but didn't move to do anything, not even the security guards. Cisco had that kind of pull in Miami. People knew who he was and didn't want to fuck with him.

Embarrassed and sobbing, as soon as I caught my breath, I quickly climbed to my feet and went to gather all of my things to leave. That motherfucker had ruined my party and I no longer wanted to be there. So I left as fast as I could without even saying good bye to everyone.

My Childhood

As a little girl in the 1990s, I grew up in Central Miami in a place called Overtown. Historically, Overtown had been a place where black people had settled into Florida and created a nice little community for themselves. It was right above downtown Miami, where a lot of Black Americans and Bahamian immigrants lived. My father Willie Wells was half-Bahamian himself. His family and friends liked to call him "Champ," and he was tall, dark and athletic with a basketball player's body and beautiful white teeth. I used to *love* seeing my father's big, broad smile.

I can't even lie; I was always a daddy's girl. When my father was around, I thought that everything was perfect. I had my mom, my dad, my brothers, my sisters and a regular family life. Although my parents had never married and my dad was not the father of my three older brothers, he still treated them like he was their father. There was no disrespect or animosity toward him, or at least not in the beginning.

I remember my family and I would sit down at the dinner table for home cooked meals and enjoy each other's company. My dad would come home from work to a hot meal every night, and I thought everything was beautiful. At the time, my father owned a local car wash and my mother Charmaine was a homemaker, who also worked on and off at a local supermarket.

My mother was short, light brown and half Nigerian with a brickhouse body, who loved to dress stylishly. With her short curly hair, she loved to wear anything that would accentuate her curves. But as an orphan from the age of eleven—when my Nigerian grandmother died of respiratory failure—my mother had been on the streets and had survived a hard-ass life. While going from house to house with no love or family, she ended up pregnant at fourteen and had three sons before she even turned twenty; my brothers Contrell, Myshion and Henry. I don't know where her father's people were; the Floyds. But just imagine a homeless half-Nigerian girl with three young children, trying to make it out on the streets of Miami on her own.

I don't know how the hell my mom ever did it. My brother's fathers sure didn't help her. You know how it is; a young lonely girl goes from one false love to the next and keeps getting kicked to the curb by hard-ass men with hard dicks, who don't give a damn. And my mother had an African accent that she would turn off and on depending on who she was speaking to stop people from trying to take advantage of her. So when my father finally came along, it was a blessing for her ... at first.

In contrast to my mother's upbringing as an abandoned, immigrant orphan, my father came from a very large family of aunts, uncles and cousins from the Bahamas *and* from the U.S. A lot of his Black America family came from a place called Pahokee in Palm Beach County. However, my father was an only child—who a lot times—showed it. My father would often drift off on his own little missions as if he had no family at all. He liked to hang out more with his friends. And he often had issues with showing us love and affection. He never told us that he loved us. We would always tell him first. Everything was tough love and hard work with my father. And he was very sneaky too. My mother thought he kept a side woman at all times.

So as I began to mature and look hard at my father

2

and at the neighborhood that we lived in, I realized that things weren't all what I thought they were. My father was *hardly* a perfect man and Overtown had become a very drug-infested and crime-riddled environment. We lived in a three-bedroom apartment in a four-story complex building, where drug addicts and chaos was everywhere. With my three older brothers; Contrell, Myshion and Henry, my mom and dad had me, my middle sister Charmaine and my baby sister Naomi. It was a family of *eight* all living in a three-bedroom apartment.

My mother and father stayed in the master bedroom, my two sisters and I were in the second room and my three older brothers were all in a third room. So it was very crowded there. But even though we didn't live in the best neighborhood with a lot of room, I felt that my family life was fine. Sure, we lived in the hood with poverty, crime and all of that, but everyday my father would get up and take us all to school and see us off with love, pride and dignity. So the poverty didn't matter to us in my younger days. We all knew we had each other.

But like a lot of parents in tough situations, my mom and dad would fight over grown-up stuff. At first, I didn't know what it was all about. But as I got older, sometimes my dad would have me around when he dealt with these other women. Not knowing any better, I would tell my mom what about it, which only caused my family more problems when she would go off on him. My mother was not having the bullshit and she was ready to fight anyone at any place or time.

Maybe that's what my father wanted to happen. I don't really know. But why would he have other women right in front of me like that? I think my father trusted me to a fault. And I wasn't trying to betray him or anything; I was only being a kid and telling my mother what I saw. I didn't even realize what cheating was all about until my mother would go crazy about it. Of course, I learned though.

I remember my mom would have some of these side chicks running down the street and ducking for cover. It was like a crazy soap opera, but it was real life for us. But no matter what, my parents still tried to work it out and stay together.

Aside of my father's issues with other women, my parents got along well with each other. They would get mad at one another and give each other space for a few days, but I thought it was impossible to keep them apart for good. Sometimes they seemed like a sister and brother with how close they were. And every other Friday or Saturday was family day, where they liked to take us all to Bayside Park to enjoy ourselves. It was an oceanfront property right next to Overtown with boats, pony ride machines, musicians performing for money and everybody walking around, eating seafood and having a good time. They even had a Hooters sports bar over there.

I remember my mom would dress us up in pretty skirts and shoes with nice cloths and really make us feel good about ourselves. I loved it when my family and I would go out together and do things. However, my innocent family life wouldn't last for long. Those grown-up issues between my parents were not going away. How long could my parents keep coming back together to work things out?

It's hard to make anything last forever. So eventually, my mom got tired of my dad with his cheating and lies, and they started fight all of the time. It got to the point where their fighting seemed like our everyday family life. And my father would leave for days at a time without us knowing where he was.

In my father's absence, my two older brothers Contrell and Myshion started acting up in the streets. They started hanging out with the other crazy teenagers from our neighborhood, and with no father figure around to stop them, there was a lot of bad things to get involved in. Like I said, drug addicts, dealers and hustlers were everywhere, and my two oldest brothers started taking advantage of criminal opportunities like so many other kids.

In those years, the old Miami Arena—where the Miami Heat basketball team used to play—was right there in Overtown, surrounded by all of these people in poverty. So these kids started robbing people and breaking into their cars and stuff during and after the games. These robberies were happening all the time. There were people getting robbed everyday at the old arena. It was like the thing to do if you wanted some fast money. And my brothers "Pat Pat"—what we called Contrell—and Shion were down with it too.

I remember this one time Shion—who was always the craziest—robbed this older teenage boy at the train stop, while we were coming home from school. It was me, Shion and my little sister Charmaine, who was named after my mother. But we just called her "Weeda."

Shion, who was short, light brown and wild with a fast temper for fighting, picked this boy out when we got off the train at our stop. He screamed at him, "What do you have in your pockets? Empty your pockets out!"

I guess my brother knew that this boy had some money on him. This boy was so terrified by my brother that he immediately emptied out his pockets. And sure enough, he had five-hundred dollars on him. So my brother snatched the money out of his hands and told my sister Weeda and me to run fast behind him.

I couldn't believe it! My brother did that shit right out in front of us, and my sister took off running right behind like he told us to. Even at a young age, my sister Weeda was down with that that, but I wasn't. I looked at this boy, who was crying about his money being stolen, and I thought that it was wrong. And this boy was older than my brother, but Shion already had a reputation in our neighborhood for being crazy, so nobody wanted to fuck with him. Even older boys were scared of him. My brother would fight anybody.

Well, I felt sorry for this boy, so I led him back to where we lived to get his money back. And what happened next, I will never forget for as long as I live.

This boy told my mother what happened with my brother taking in his money from him at the train station, and my mother went inside and got his money back. But when this boy left our house with his money, my mother whipped my *ass*!

She told me, "You don't *ever* do no shit like that. You don't bring someone back to our *house*. You don't know what he could have done. He could have gotten your brother arrested, killed and *anything*. You don't know who he could come back with. And now this boy knows where we live."

I guess my mother had a point to a certain degree, especially in our neighborhood. That boy could have shot our whole house up if he had a gun or something. I thought I had done a good thing by getting this boy his money back. But evidently safety, survival and family came *first*. So I learned my lesson *early* not to talk or snitch on anyone, especially not my family members. I still knew it wasn't right to steal though.

I can't say the same about my sister Weeda. She seemed to like that drama shit and she was constantly telling people, "I'll get my brother on you."

Shion kicked a couple of boy's asses for my sister. But I never liked that stuff, so I tried my best to avoid it. I would rather not even say that someone was bothering me than to get my brothers involved. I thought that they would eventually *kill* somebody. So I just didn't do it. I didn't want to be bothered with all of that.

But when my father wasn't around, my brothers had

to do what *he* used to do for us. They were walking us to school and picking us up, helping to feed us at home when my mom had to work late and even helping us to do our homework. My oldest brother Contrell even cooked for us sometimes. But as they got older and started getting into more trouble, I could no longer count on my brothers to be around either. I would wake up with them one day and they would be gone the next.

Contrell, who we called "Pat Pat" for some reason, was very moody and selfish at times. Sometimes it seemed like everything was about *him*, as if he didn't have a family. That reminded me a lot of my father Willie. And at first, when Pat Pat and Shion would go out and do what they did in the streets, robbing and burglarizing people for money, they did it to help my mother out. They didn't want to see us all struggling with no money and no father in the house. And like I said, there father's weren't helping anyone.

Myshion's father had been in jail for *forever* and Contrell's father was killed at a Miami night club after some kind of an argument. So my brothers took it upon themselves to do whatever they needed to do to help my mother to pay the bills and for groceries to keep her household. But once Pat Pat started getting big money and dealing in drugs and whatnot, he would keep more of it to himself and break bread more with his *friends* than with his family. That's what led to Contrell's first big arrest, when one of his friends snitched on him after getting caught in a burglary attempt when my brother could have taken Shion with him. And it had nothing to do with him trying to protect his little brother from committing a crime. It had all to do with Contrell wanting to make his own moves outside of his family. And he paid for it with incarceration time at Florida prison boot camp.

The next thing I knew, both of my oldest brothers were in and out of detention centers and boot camps.

They were not even out of high school yet with long rap sheets on their records. So Contrell would get out of for six months or whatever, while Myshion was still locked up, and by the time Shion would get out. Pat Pat would be on his way back in. Then they would be locked up together for three and five years at a time for various burglary, drug possession and hustling charges. And my mother was constantly running back and forth to the Florida courthouses to save their asses.

She was always telling the judge, "I'll take care of them. They won't do this again."

But I knew better than that shit. My brothers couldn't wait to get back out on the streets to commit their next caper. Once you get involved in that cycle of making fast and crazy money like that, it's hard to *stop*. Where else were they going to get that kind of fast money? So I felt bad for my mother and for *all* of us to keep losing our brothers to the prison system like that. We couldn't even share a holiday together as a family anymore.

Whenever my brothers were out of their incarceration, they would take me, my sisters and my brother Henry to the circus, to basketball games and all of that. But most of the time one or the other was still locked up. Until eventually, the judge threw the book at Contrell and gave his ass a twenty-year sentence in jail, after he got arrested and snitched on by the same damn friend who did it to him before. Some people just don't learn their lessons. Nevertheless, my mother tried to protect her sons every time.

It was *horrible* situation to be in as a child and I was devastated by it. Our family was being torn apart right in front of my eyes. My dad and my brothers were constantly in and out of my life, and there was nothing that I could do about it, nor could I count on them anymore. My grades started to slip in school because it and I lost a lot of my confidence and self-esteem. I just felt like something

8

bad was always about to happen to us. Even when my parents would try to get back together something would always happen.

I remember they had another big fight in our living room. By that time, my father was in and out of our house, like a rolling stone. We had no idea what he was doing from one day to next, or if he really wanted to stay with us at all. It was like he testing my mother to see how bad she wanted him back. So they got into a big fight again—probably over another woman—and my mother, at fight feet-two, tried to fight my dad. Well, with him standing over six-feet tall, it wasn't much of a fight.

She was screaming, "Motherfucker, I'll kill you!" and all of that.

But my father grabbed her by the neck to restrain her and hold her away from him. That's when my brother Shion ran into the kitchen and pulled out a short, black knife to protect my mother with.

My brother screamed, "Let go of my mom! Get off of my mom!"

With Myshion being as crazy as he was, I thought that he would actually *stab* my father. So we were screaming and yelling and all kinds of stuff for them all to stop fighting. This is when Contrell was already locked up, and Shion still wasn't old enough or big enough to really fight my father like that. So my dad grabbed the knife from him and held it up to my mom neck. That's when things really got tense. We didn't know if he was ready to stab her and kill her right there in front of us or what. We were all in shock, screaming and yelling and praying that my dad would calm down and not kill her. It was all just ... *crazy*!

My baby sister Naomi screamed out, "NOOOO!" and burst into tears. You know, she was only like five or six-years old when all of this was happening.

Finally, my father stopped, put the knife down and just walked away from it all without hurting anyone. He walked out of the house and just kept on going. Then my mom ran out after him and started throwing the rest of his clothes and stuff out on the steps.

"And you take all your shit with you and just *get out*!" she screamed at him. But my father was already gone by then. He didn't have that much stuff left at our house anyway. And that was it. My father would never live with us again. My mother even changed our last names from my father's name of Wells to her father's last name of Floyd, like my older brothers had.

I remember that was right around the time that my brother Henry's father was killed in an attempted robbery. Henry's father was trying to get away when the robbers shot him. People were always getting killed where we lived. But Henry's father was the only one who actually tried to do something for his son. He would give Henry money all the time and buy him things, so Henry never got involved with the street life like my older brothers. Henry had a good father, but that didn't help the rest of us. We weren't that man's children. So we all considered Henry *spoiled* and he would complain about not getting new bikes and things that *none* of us got.

Henry actually thought he was *deprived* because of that, like he was always supposed to get things that we couldn't get.

I was like, "Who the hell you think *you* are?" None of us were getting special treatment. My father had just moved out for *good* and I felt like we had been orphaned and abandoned like my mother had. I felt like my father didn't love us anymore, and he was a big part of my family life. So once he left, there was a giant hole in my heart that no one could fill. And I think I took it worse than anyone else did because I was my father's first child and the oldest daughter.

It was all up to my mother to raise us after that; to feed us, clothe us, discipline us, send us all to school and everything. That's when she became our mother *and* our father. And when we didn't clean up the house like she told us to, she began to beat us. We weren't getting out of discipline just because my father was no longer around. But it was a heavy load on my mother to raise us all by herself. So it was hard to blame her for what she had to accept for us to survive.

She would wake up sometimes enraged. "Oh my God! This house is *mess*. You have to clean it up. Clean it up *right now* before I beat your asses!" And we would all scramble around to do what she told us to.

Looking back on it, I couldn't blame my mother for anything. Without a father in the house, we were not doing what we were supposed to do. We were not even cleaning up the house. We couldn't expect our mother to do everything. So she started wearing our asses out on the regular. And we deserved it too.

Then the neighbors called the police on my mother and told them that she was abusing us. I don't know why they would do that. My mother was just trying to hold down her household in the middle of chaos like any other parent. But like twenty police officers showed at our house up and banged on our door with officials from the child protection and human resource services with them. We just called them the HRS, and these officials from child services started questioning me, my little sisters and my brother Henry. At that time, Contrell and Myshion were both out of the house in detention centers and boot camps.

"Did she hit you? Did she hurt you? Does she beat you?" they asked us over and over again.

What they were asking us was *crazy*. It was like they were trying to put thoughts and words in our heads to make us turn against our mother so they take her away from us. My mom had to discipline us like any other mother, but that didn't mean she was *abusing* us. She loved

11

us, cared for us and tried to give us the best that she could. But she was on her own with four young kids to raise and it had overwhelmed her.

With all that was going on, my youngest brother Henry caved into the pressure from these people and started to agree with them. He told them that my mother *had* abused him, which was a *lie*. My mother would *never* do that. She was always encouraging and supportive of anything that had to do with her kids, and she would always give us her all. So these accusations about her abusing us were all unbelievable.

The police took our mother away in handcuffs and held her at their squad cars. Then they told us they would take her away from us for *good* and she may not ever come back. It all felt like a bad movie. I remember my mother breaking down and crying in front of us. My mother just couldn't *believe* that her own child had turned against her like that as everyone in our neighborhood watched it. And I was so *angry* with Henry after he did that. I felt like it was all my brother's fault for going along with their plans. The boy was just *spoiled* like that. It was all about him that day.

Our mother being taken away like that was a very disturbing scene for *any* children and family to go through. Then the police officers and HRS officials called my father and told him to come and get us or to send a family member to get us, while they threatened to take us all into HRS custody for child services.

I felt that my dad had left us all in that situation to rot. Then he showed up and took us all to his Grandmother Mae Bell's house in Miami Lakes. Mae Bell was a tall, light brown Christian-type woman, who liked to wear wigs. She was my great grandmother on my father's maternal side, and they were all from Pahokee. My father's paternal side was from the Bahamas.

In Miami Lakes, Mae Bell had a townhouse in a much more prestigious neighborhood, mixed with blacks, whites, Hispanic and lots of pretty green lawns. People had a lot more money there than in Overtown. But Mae Bell and her family didn't have money like that; they just had that house. I don't know how she got it, but she had a lot of different family members living there; her two daughters, nieces, nephews, grandchildren and great grandchildren. Then my father added us to the mix.

We knew some of the people in the house but we were never really spent any time with them. We were still kids who had never been around everyone. So my brother Henry, Weeda and Naomi were all like, "Who are all these *people* in her house?"

Like I said, we didn't spend enough time with them to know them well. They didn't have even room for us in there. A lot of times the house was unclean and it was always noisy, and none of us wanted to be there. They weren't even related to my brother Henry, so you know he didn't want to be there. And the only clothes we had were what we brought from my mother's house that day.

A few days later when my mother was able come back and see us at my great grandmother's house, we were all happy to see her. Even my brother Henry was happy to see her after he had falsified those reports to the HRS officials. He knew that what he had done was wrong. My mother would never abuse my brother or *any* of us. So when she walked through the door, our eyes lit up like it was Christmas. She brought us food, new clothes and most of all a mother's love, which we had all missed.

The whole time that we there in that crowded house with my father's people, they didn't really have any love for us. How could they? We were a bunch of extra mouths to feed and my brother Henry was not even my father's child. My father had a new girlfriend that he was seeing and everything.

Well, when my mother walked into the house to get us, my father came out to greet her from where he was

13

upstairs with his new girlfriend, and my mother handed him a letter that she had written.

I had no idea what was in her letter, but I sure remember my mother handing it to him. For whatever reason, her letter seemed very important to her and she wanted to hand it to him as soon as she saw him.

My father took the letter, read it and asked my mother to follow him to talk to her in private, but she refused to go with him. Instead, she told us what she found out, while my father waited downstairs for her *enraged*. My mother told us that she had found out from the HRS officials that my father was asking for full custody of all of his children. That was what her letter was about. She was asking my father why he was trying to take her children away from her.

My father heard my mother telling us everything she knew, while he kept trying to get her attention. He wanted her to talk to him about it and not to us, but my mother continued to ignore him. That's when my father pulled back his huge fist and punched my mother square in her face.

I had never seen a man hit a woman like that before. Blood started shooting out of my mother's nose like it was raining or something. Her blood looked like a bloody, red water faucet and I was in *shock*. We were *all* in shock, especially my baby sister Naomi. She started screaming, yelling, crying and having a fit, more than the rest of us. It was really traumatic for her.

As my mother tried to cover it up with her hands to hide her face, her blood started dripping through her fingers and all over the floor. I had never seen that much blood in my life. Before we knew it, the whole floor was red, covered in my mother's fresh blood.

My brother Henry took off for the front door and started yelling for the neighbors to call the police. But it was his ass and his *lies* that put us all in that situation in the first place. Without Henry's bullshit—agreeing with those officials from the HRS—we would have never even been there with my father's family. Or at least that's how I was thinking. So I was still very bitter toward my brother.

When the police finally arrived at my great grandmother's townhouse, my father's family tried to hide everything and cover up for him. They tried to clean up the blood and everything. My great grandmother Mae Bell even tried to lie to the police, claiming that the blood had come from her stubbing her toe. Do you believe that shit? I couldn't believe she even said that. She was lying right there in front of us. I couldn't respect her anymore after that. I understood that my dad was her grandson and that she didn't want the police to take him away, but after seeing my dad punch my mother like that, I felt that he *deserved* to be taken away and handcuffed. I felt that no woman should be hit like that by a man, *especially* not my mother.

Well, the police didn't believe their lies about what happened either and they took my father away to jail. I don't know what really happened with my father's case, but he was back out on the streets within days. They probably gave him some kind of probation or whatever. So my mom took us back and moved us out to this area called Miami Gardens in North Miami near Carol City.

And I'll tell you what, my dad was lucky that my two brothers Contrell and Myshion were not around to see that, because they would had *killed* my father that day. Unfortunately, my brothers had already been locked up for countless charges of doing craziness themselves. What else could you expect from unloved and unguided teenage boys in a chaotic family situation like ours in Miami? It was the same story for a lot of young black people in that area.

To be honest, I was still too young to understand everything that was going on with my family. At the time, my dad was putting a lot of pressure on my mother with all that was happening to us. He told my mother that he didn't tell the HRS that he wanted full custody. He said that the agency was lying to make her sweat. Not only that, but the Florida court system already knew my mother because of my two oldest brothers being locked up so much.

But my mother still didn't believe my father. And after he broke her nose like that, she needed to wear a mask over her face for several months to heal it. He had also broken her pride. With no family of her own and nowhere to go, who did my mother have to protect her? So she was forced to be strong and deal with it. But she was very hurt by everything my father and his family had done to her, because she had always trusted him. Although they had their fights over other women, she felt that my father would never try to hurt her or allow anyone to take her kids away from her like they were trying to do. So she felt the ultimate betrayal from him. My father had pulled the final straw.

Not only that, but my baby sister Naomi was now traumatized by everything. She was so terrified of my father that she didn't want to be anywhere *near* him. And she started acting out and having fits every time anyone even raised their voice or acted aggressively toward my mother. Naomi would just *loose it*. She had these reoccurring thoughts of people trying to hurt my mother. That's part of the reason why she had to move to North Miami to get away from Overtown. My sister even had psychological evaluations and family counseling after that. We *all* had to go to counseling.

For the longest time, I had so much anger toward my father. It took me *years* to want to be around him again. I still couldn't believe that he had done that to my mom. But that's how angry they were at each other and how brutal their fights had become. So it was no going back after that, even for friendship.

Then we had to keep going back and forth to court about my mother's child abuse case that my brother Henry had helped them to believe. That left some scars of distrust in me that I would have for the rest of my life. I felt like I couldn't trust or depend on anyone, including my own family. I had like this love and hate relationship with my father from that point on. I just felt like my true love for him would never be the same.

I remember I would be afraid to even go to school sometimes because I would think that my dad would be there to pick me up and I didn't want to see him. My fear of him wasn't as bad as my baby sister Naomi, but I felt same way she did at times.

All the while, the HRS officials were still trying to split our family up and take us away from our mother, but she wouldn't let them. She let them know that she had moved us out to North Miami and Miami Gardens, where it was a much better environment than in Overtown. Overtown may have been historical for black people, but it was no longer a safe place for us to live, especially without a father around to protect us and guide his children. And although my mother was a small, single mom, she found a way to keep fighting for her kids. She was still doing housekeeping, grocery jobs and even hanging off the back of garbage trucks, emptying trash cans with the men. She did anything to provide for us.

However, the socials services people from the HRS kept checking in with my mother because of Henry. She had a record for child abuse now, so my mother had to watch everything she did with us and she could never put her hands on Henry again. Different people were always checking up my mom, as if they had *spies* on her or something.

So she would just tell Henry, "You can go ahead and go. Do what you want to do."

My brothers Pat Pat and Shion even threatened to

whip Henry's ass when they heard about that shit. But they were both away in detention centers or whatever when it happened. So they never really had the time to deal with Henry like that.

Henry was never in trouble out in streets like they were. He was like a little school boy. But then he started slacking off in his studies too. He kept feeling like he was being mistreated after that, like someone was always out to get him. But he brought that shit on himself. He was the one who didn't want to take any responsibility for his actions. He respected my mom, but he was always catching little attitudes with her around the house and acting rebellious. My mom even sent his ass to boot camp for a year and Henry *hated* that. But my mom couldn't let that boy get away with anything he wanted. Henry had rules in the house like everyone else.

Once my mom worked out visitations terms with my father again, he would come and get me and Weeda and take us to his new house in an area called Liberty City, where he lived with this evil-ass woman named Vanessa. She was slightly taller than my mom, dark-skinned and was overweight. And she never wanted us around. But my father would often leave me and Charmaine at their house with this woman anyway. However, my baby sister Naomi never went there with us. She still couldn't take being around my father. It would be many years later before she would even talk to him.

So me and Weeda would go over to my father's house without Henry or Naomi, and I remember I would *beg* him, "Please, *please* don't leave us here with this woman."

It was a two-bedroom house and every time we went over there, there was some kind of altercation. Their house was real raggedy, rundown and always dirty. My sister and I even had to spend the night sometimes, where we would always sleep on the hard living-room floor with like one or two blankets, while Vanessa and my dad slept in the master bedroom and her two kids slept in the other room.

She had a boy and a girl and she wouldn't even let us sleep in their rooms. I'm talking about this woman had *no* love for us. We were just in the way of what she really wanted, which was my *father* all to herself. But my father would leave us there with her anyway. He was a grown man with things to do. So when he ran his errands or whatever, this woman Vanessa would constantly mistreat us, her *and* her family.

I was only eleven-years-old when he first started taking us around this woman, and my sister Charmaine was ten. And every time my sister and I went over to visit their house, Vanessa would verbally abuse us, calling us dumb bitches and telling us that we would never be shit. She would call my mom a slut, a hoe and all kinds of shit. This woman would say *anything* to us.

I was like, "Where is my dad?" I mean, wasn't what a father was supposed to do, protect their children from adults mistreating them like that? I was eleven-years-old! I questioned why he would my leave us over there. It seemed like every time my dad came to get us to bring us to his house with Vanessa, this woman would try to kick him out, *him* and us.

Vanessa would then make up all kinds of lies to get our father angry at us. She wanted to make our lives a living hell, to the point where she taped signs to the bathroom doors calling us "nasty-ass bitches," "you ain't shit" and "clean up the fucking bathroom."

She even created fake sex letters and gave them to my father as if my sister and I had written them. "Oh my God, look what I found from your daughters."

I was like, *Really? At ten and eleven-years-old, we're writing sex letters? Why would we even do that?* I wasn't thinking about sex. I couldn't *believe* what my sister and I were going through with my father and this woman. The worse part about it was that it *worked*. My father was constantly taking this woman's side for shit.

I warned my father about this crazy-ass woman as soon as she started mistreating us. But all she would do was deny it, every single time. I don't remember my father taking our side of the story even once. Every time my sister and I would tell him what she did or said, he would go and ask her about it and come back to us.

"She told she didn't do that. She said she didn't say that."

It was *ridiculous*. Vanessa was always cursing at us and acting belligerent. But it was always her word against *ours* and my father never took our side of the story. My dad was just ignoring the facts even though he saw some of her signs and he *knew* that she always used foul language around us. Then he told me one time to record her saying stuff. Do you believe that?

I'm like, *I'm eleven-years-old! I'm a child!* Why should I have to record someone when I'm telling you that she's mistreating me? Why would a father do that to his daughter?

I was my father's first born and oldest child, so I continued to take his actions harder than everyone else. That's why my self-esteem took a big hit. I was tired of being beaten down mentally, physically and psychologically. And this woman was constantly competing with our mother too. From the moment we met Vanessa, she was always asking us questions about our mom and family just so she could use it against us.

My father even tried to play head games with us. He would ask me, "Don't you want to see me happy? Your *mother* has someone else. Don't you want me to have someone?"

But I saw nothing attractive about this woman at all. No one liked going to her house and no one was happy there. Was that the best that my father could do?

When I turned thirteen, I had finally given up on it. I didn't want to go to my dad's house anymore at all. What was the point of it, just to be mistreated and lied on again, while this woman plotted against us? I still wanted to see my father, but not if Vanessa had to be involved. She was even nasty on our phone calls to our father.

We would call over to her house to speak to him sometimes and she would hang up the phone on us. Sometimes she would say, "Stop playing on my damn phone." Or "Don't disrespect me when you call here." She only did that to stop us from speaking to our father. This woman was really *crazy* like that.

I'm not saying that it was right, but one time I cursed back at her. I said, "Fuck you, you fat-ass *bitch*! I'm not *playing* on your phone." I was just tired of her bullshit.

I told my mother, "I *refuse* to go over there anymore. I'm not going anywhere near that woman."

I figured if my father really wanted to see us, then he could come to us. I was like, *Fuck my dad and Vanessa!* I got to the point where it was either her or me. And he chose *her.* So be it.

And do you know that after all we went through with Vanessa, my father still married that woman? None of his children were even invited to the wedding. How could you not have your own *children* at your wedding? What kind of father or family would do that? That's how much that woman despised us. Well, we didn't care about her either.

In my own cynical way, I was actually *happy* that my father had married Vanessa. I figured he would get *all* that he deserved from that woman when he began to find out the *truth* of how hateful, deceitful and just how *evil* she was.

Around that same time, my mother started calling me "Dior." I had no idea where that came from, so I immediately asked her about it.

"*Dior*? Mom, why are you calling me that?"

She said, "Because you are acting very *golden*. You think that you're *special*." My mother thought that I had a certain *air* about me, like I deserved a better life than what we had. And I *did* think way. I thought we *all* deserved a better life, just like my brother Henry did.

This was all while my mother was still going through hard times. I remember we tried to move into a new home in North Miami and the landlord took my mother's money and disappeared, leaving us homeless. No one ever heard from this man again. He didn't even return to the property, and my mother was broken-hearted and crying. So she had to get the money from my brothers out in the streets again. That was another reason why my brothers were so wild like that. It was a like a do or die situation for us.

By that time, I was in middle school and we were moving around a lot. We moved from once place to the next in North Miami, Miami Gardens, North Miami Beach and back to the North Miami again. But it was all better than going back to Overtown. When we moved to the North Miami area, they had a lot of Haitian immigrants and Hispanics there. A lot of them were hardworking house keepers and domestics, like my mom. They were not as violent as the people who lived in Overtown with the drug dealers, addicts and burglars and stuff, so I liked it much better up north.

However, my two older brothers would get out of doing time and go right back to Overtown and Brownsville, where they still knew people and would get into trouble. They called Brownsville "Brown Sub" for some reason. That's where my brother Contrell set up his first big drug house.

He and Shion weren't allowed to stay with us anymore, because my mother couldn't afford their bullshit and they still didn't want to do right. My brothers started getting into home invasions and crazy stuff like that. And if the HRS people came around while they were out there robbing people again, we would have *all* been in trouble. We could have lost our mom and family *forever* because of my brothers. So after years of trying to beat and threaten my brothers with mops and broomsticks, my mother just couldn't do it anymore and she kicked them out to do their dirt on their own. She would still go down to the courtrooms and beg the judges for them; she just didn't allow them to live with us.

That gave my brother Pat Pat even more reason to act selfish with his money. At this Brownsville house where he stayed, he was making *thousands* of dollars a night and still didn't feel obligated to help out his mother as much as he *used* to. It was like, making more money made him greedier and stingier. He was always saying he had less money than what we *thought* he had, as if he was holding back on us.

Pat Pat had moved up to a top drug-dealer position in our old neighborhood and was holding his own against some of the older hustlers. He was dark and stocky with a low haircut and a beard that made him look older and rougher. But he was only seventeen or eighteen in a grown man's business, and he was running things. My brother had spent plenty of time in boot camps and juvenile detention centers, so he was hard enough to ignore the threats and intimidation of the older hustlers. They were constantly telling him not sell drugs to customers on certain street corners. That's what drug dealers do. It's always about territory.

That was when I started hearing about everything my brother would do on the streets. I even caught him in a drug transaction at his apartment one time, where he wasn't expecting me. And once he started making big money like that, everything changed about him, and I didn't like it. But he was still my big brother and I still wanted to see him sometimes. So I surprised when I decided to show up at his place and he was real upset that I had caught him.

He started yelling and cursing at me. "Girl, what the fuck are you doing here?! Get out of here. This ain't no place for you. Get out!"

He told his big, bodyguard and worker to take me away and out of the room. I was in shock, but I didn't know what to do about it. I mean, I knew that it was wrong and everything, but he was still my brother. By that time, Contrell had assault weapons and shotguns all up in his living room in plain sight, so you could see that he meant business. And it was no surprise that he was headed to jail again for a long time. He didn't even have the decency to hide what he was doing anymore. It was like, we wasn't his family at all. And he ended up trusting the same dude who had snitched on him for robbery and sent him to boot camp. This time, his same so-called friend snitched on him for drug selling and got my brother sentenced to twenty years in prison.

That didn't make any sense to me at *all* to trust someone like that over your own family. But those were all the things I had to go through during the first years of my life. So by the time I became a teenager, I was pretty much an angry and confused child, who had seen and been through much more than I should have. And I was still desperately looking for love.

No Time For Boys

When I reached fourteen-years-old, I started to attend Miami Jackson Senior High School in Liberty City. It was about five minutes away from my father's house, where he still lived with Vanessa and her two children. But by that time, I barely saw or spoke to my father. We had nothing to talk about. I understood that I had to move on with my own life without him, and my life was more peaceful that way. However, deep down inside, I still wanted that fatherly love like any other daughter.

I was only fourteen, but I was very mature and advanced for my age. I had already been through a lot and I was basically the most dependable child in my household. My two oldest brothers were no longer there and Henry was not mature at *all* in my opinion. He was still being very defiantly to my mother and he was not adding much to our household. So that left me—as the next in line—as the most reliable.

My mother tried as best she could to give me all of the love and support that she could offer, but somehow it just wasn't enough. I admit that even at a young age, I wanted a *man's* love. I wanted to feel *needed* as a young woman and my mother couldn't provide that feeling for me. Maybe I had been around too many grown-up issues too early in my life, but that was how I felt at the time.

The bus ride to Jackson Senior High School was two hours long from where I lived with my mother in North Miami Beach. My mother wanted me to go there because she was more familiar with the neighborhood and still knew the teachers and everything. A lot of her friend's children went to Jackson Senior High School and she felt more comfortable with her baby girl being there than in North Miami where she didn't know anyone. And every day when I headed to school and climbed off the Metro bus, I would bump into this older guy named Travis. He was in his early twenties and would always stop me and try to give me his number, but he wasn't my type.

I hadn't really started dating yet, but I *knew* that I didn't want to talk to Travis. He was around the same short height as my older brothers and looked on the rough side with cornrolls and crooked teeth. I was not interested in this boy at *all*, but to stop him from bothering me every day, I took his number with no plans of ever calling him.

When I turned fifteen, I remember walking back from getting my hair done at the salon on a Sunday afternoon. I was headed toward the bus stop, wearing a pink and white Rocawear tennis set with my hair blow-dried out like the singer Aaliyah. I was looking good, feeling good and strutting down the street like with my long, brown legs when this gray Ford Focus pulled up beside me near the bus stop with tinted windows. The windows were so dark, I could hardly see who was in the car.

This young black man rolled down his window from inside and asked if he could talk to me. But I backed away on the sidewalk. There was no way I was approaching some stranger in a dark car like that. He could have been trying to do *anything*. But he spoke to me with confidence with his car parked at the curb. Then he got out and sat with me on the bench at the bus stop.

He said, "Hi, my name is Louis. I've been seeing you around, walking with your sisters and mom and I always thought you were beautiful. You live off one-forty-Fifth Street, right?"

He knew where I lived and everything. I was

impressed. I said, "Yeah, so you've been watching me, hunh?" I was flattered too.

He smiled and said, "I never bothered you because I knew you were young. But you're getting older now. I want to give you my number to call me."

Louis must have thought that I was older than fifteen. Louis was nineteen, but he had the boyish looks of an older high-schooler. He was very dark and handsome with acne scars on his face, but it didn't bother me and he didn't sweat it either. He wrote his number down on a piece of paper for me to call him. Then he sped off into the streets like it was nothing. He didn't hang around to try and convince me to call him or anything. So I was very curious about him and wanted to know more.

I jumped on the Metro bus and couldn't stop from thinking about him. I could imagine myself caressing Louis's dark, chocolate body and his scared face. So as soon as I got off the bus and in the house, I called him from my mom's house phone. She was strict about what I did and who I talked to, but at a certain point, she had to trust me. She knew that I wasn't sexually active at the time.

We only spoke briefly, but we agreed to meet again that next night after school. So that Monday morning, I got dressed excitedly and rode the bus to and from school, anticipated my first official date with Louis that evening after school.

I don't know what I was thinking to invite this older man to pick me up from in front of my mother's house on my first date as a teenager, but that's just what I did.

Louis pulled up to my house in his gray Ford Focus and walked up to the front door to greet me and my mother, while I blushed in the background and got ready. Louis was very respectful to my mother so she liked him too. She didn't mind me going out with him. Every girl has to start dating at some time, so she let him take me out with a strict curfew.

27

"*Dior*, you be back in this house when you're supposed to be," my mother told me. She seemed to always call me Dior whenever I did something grown, defiant or sassy. So my sisters and brother started to do the same thing. I guess they all thought it was funny.

Anyway, I walked out with Louis and climbed into his car, feeling special on my first official date. We ended up driving out to Williams Lehman Park in North Miami and sitting side by side in the front seat of his car. Even though Louis was slightly older than me, we clicked immediately and I got him to open up to me about his life. He seemed distraught about his family and only talked about his sister Linda. He didn't even say anything else about his mother, so I assumed that they didn't have a good relationship.

I was attract to Louis from day one, so I leaned over to kiss him and lift up his oversized black shirt to caress his chest, as if I knew what I was doing. But as I caressed his chest with my fingers, I felt several wounds and was surprised by it. I looked down and saw that they were bullet wounds. I didn't freak out about it but it was weird to touch. They were fleshy wounds that didn't even feel like they were healed all the way. So I pulled his shirt back down.

Louis said, "Somebody tried to kill me and shot up this other car I had. And I got hit with three or four bullets."

He never told me what he was involved in, who shot at him or *why* and I didn't really ask him about it. I didn't want to judge him or jump to any conclusions either. All I knew was that I was enjoyed his company and he was treated me like a queen. So I listened to him as he told me all the things he wanted about his life. We sat just in the car at Lehman Park, looking out at the skyline of the city as the ocean waves came in. It was a real peaceful date and my first ever.

Caught up in the moment of his company, I nearly missed my mother's curfew as Louis rushed to get me back home in time. And after he left me that night, I couldn't stop thinking about him and his life and how he had been shot at. He could have been killed before I even met him. So I began to think that we were meant to be.

Louis was a real sweetheart who knew just how to contain his anger around me. I knew that he had been into things out in the street life, but he didn't show that with me. I got to see his sensitive side, the *real* Louis without him having to act crazy on anyone to prove his manhood. Once I got used to his phone calls, where he would always check up on me, suddenly two days turned into two weeks without me hearing from him. Then two weeks turned into two months, before the months became a year.

Louis just disappeared, leaving me broken-hearted again. I felt like the men I loved would always be taken away from me and I couldn't understand why.

In the meantime, Travis kept popping up and hounding me to call him as often as he could.

"Hey girl, I gave you my number three times now. When are you gonna call me."

The man just wouldn't take a hint and stop bothering me. I wished that *he* was the one to disappear. Other guys my age tried to talk to me too, all throughout high school. I had a banging body for my young age, so all of the boys wanted to talk to me, including the football and basketball players. They would give me their numbers and try to walk me to the bus stop, offer to take me home and anything they could to get my attention. But I still wasn't interested in any of them. I didn't have time for boys.

I tried to stay away from a lot of young guys who went to school with me on purpose, because they liked to talk too much about the girls they had been with at school and had given girls bad reputations. I was around far too much high school gossip about who was fucking who, all up and down the hallways and after school, and I didn't like it, nor did I trust any of those guys not to run their mouth to people. So I chose not to deal with them at all. I had no time for that bullshit with young boys. I chose to deal with men.

When I turned sixteen, I finally transferred back to my neighborhood high school at North Miami Beach. And I don't know if Travis followed me there, or asked someone about where I transferred or what, because he popped back up, hounding me again.

He chased me down as I walked home from school one day, and he already had his number written down on a piece of paper.

He pressed it into my hand and said, "Girl, you need to call me and stop bullshitting."

I must admit, the man sure was persistent. But maybe I should have read that as a clear warning sign of what was to come. Travis was not willing to leave me alone. Nevertheless, I finally called him anyway.

Even though he was not my type, I called and talked to Travis mainly about my life, my brothers going back and forth to jail and all about my father's wife Vanessa and how she had mistreated us when we were younger. I was just talking about my problems for the most part. I didn't have anything else to say to him. And I *surely* didn't want to know anything about him. But little did I know that I would eventually let this man into my life and he would turn things completely upside down.

Travis kept popping up in my neighborhood, and I became used to him. You know, when a person is always around you like that, whether you like them or not, you become familiar. It wasn't as he was a stranger anymore, I just didn't like him the way he liked me. But Travis kept begging me to go out with him until I finally gave in.

Up to that point, I still hadn't been with a guy

sexually. I wasn't really seeing anyone and I didn't have any crushes. So I guess Travis caught me at the right time. And the difference the between him and Louis was that Travis was trying to fuck me on the first night, where Louis really wanted to get to know me and talk to me.

I drove around shotgun with Travis in his 1998 turquoise blue Ford Thunderbird, while listening to Trick Daddy's new single, *Thug's Holiday*, blasting through the car speakers. I finally felt comfortable around the man. He still wasn't my type, but he was there to be with, you know. Sometimes it happens like that.

The next thing I knew, we were pulling up at a cheap hotel in Hialeah, about thirty-five to forty minutes south from where I lived in North Miami. He had planned to take me far enough away where it would be hard for me to get back home easily. Then he insisted that we were just going to go in to chill, but any girl knows better than that. This older man was a *freak* and he had been waiting for *years* to get me alone like that. Nevertheless, I followed him inside anyway. It wasn't as if I was scared of him or anything. Like I said, I had become used to Travis.

We walked up into the room, and it was a no-thrills place with cheap furniture and a plain bed with all white sheets that I felt was beneath me. Even at a young age, I felt that I deserved the best, including a better hotel room to chill in. I had never even been in a hotel room before, but I knew from TV and the movies that were a lot better than that one. But Travis didn't care. He just saw it as a cheap come-up to get some pussy from a hot young girl that he had been sweating. And I was all new to it. I hadn't even had sex before.

Once we were inside the room, Travis didn't waste time with what he *really* wanted. Instead of us just chilling, he immediately started to kiss me and suck on my neck, while caressing me. I wasn't really into it at first, but I was also a sixteen-year-old girl with a natural curiosity about

31

sex, especially after Louis had gone away without giving me the love that I wanted from him. In reality, Louis should have been my first love in bed, but it didn't happen that way. I was up in the room with Travis and he wanted me.

Travis was ready to do *anything* to get my young, tight pussy. He even got on his knees and began to kiss inside my legs, licking me all the way up in between my thighs. That shit sent *chills* down my spine and in all of the right places. I had never felt that way before and never been alone like that with a man.

The next thing I knew, Travis had worked his way up to my panties which were soaking wet with excitement. I didn't even know what was happening to me, but I was getting more excited by the second. That's when Travis pulled my wet panties to the side with his fingers and stuck his wet tongue so far up my young pussy that I almost fainted.

Travis had me pent down on the bed where I couldn't move, while he licked up and down and in and out of my young pussy hole until my body started to shake and shiver out of control. And oh *God*, it felt so *good*! I couldn't believe it. The man had his tongue all up inside me and was turning my young ass *out*.

Finally, Travis climbed back up from his knees with a wet face from licking my wet pussy and he went to put a condom on his big dick. I looked down and saw how big his dick was and wondered how he would get that huge thing inside of my little pussy hole. But as wet as my pussy was from him licking and sucked it, his big dick slid right the hell in. And just like that, I was conquered.

I had no idea how being fucked or made love to would feel, but Travis had been very passionate with me up to that point. So I liked it. Once he had his dick inside me, he pushed it in deeper, big and hard as I felt a lot of discomfort. But I didn't have to feel it for long, because after like two minutes of pushing and pumping, Travis bust a big fat nut and was done with me.

I was shocked that I had lost my virginity in a cheap hotel room like that. And with Travis only lasting two minutes made it *worse*, because it felt so quick and thoughtless. It was like we were two squirrels fucking in a tree with no substance to it. So I started rushing to leave.

I guess Travis felt a little guilty about it too. So saw that I was panicking and looking disoriented. He was like, "Aw, baby, are you okay?" trying to smooth things all out.

I paid him no mind and rushed inside the bathroom and cleaned myself up. I still didn't like Travis that much and I didn't feel like chilling with him inside that cheap hotel room. And when I walk out from the bathroom I told him that I was ready to go. End of story. He didn't even argue with me because he had already gotten the pussy.

What can I say? I ended up dating Travis for a few years because of the convenience of it. He had already fucked me and had stolen my virginity, so I kept giving in to him instead of sleeping around with other guys. I knew that most of them only wanted some pussy anyway, so what was the use in even talking to them? I saw young guys as trivial. They didn't even know what they were doing with their lives yet.

I really wanted Louis, but he was no longer there for me. And since Travis was my first and only, I felt like it was his pussy. So even though I was never crazy in love with him, I remained loyal, dedicated, foolish and young. Other guys couldn't even tempt me. As far as I was concerned, I was a kept woman and I didn't think anything of it. I even began to think it was love. Travis sure acted like he was in love with me, or he was more like possessed or something.

Before I knew what was happening between us, Travis became very possessive, attitudinal and enraged all because he couldn't control me like he wanted to. I felt like he was becoming too pressed about my time and the things that I wanted to do. But I was still a teenager with girlfriends, high school sports, parties and everything else that I wanted to experience. I didn't want to stay around in the house, waiting around for him to get me. He must have been *crazy*. My mom couldn't even control me like that and we lived together. That's why she kept calling me Dior to ostracize me.

On this one morning when Travis was driving me to school, he asked me if he could see my cell phone. But that was my private property, so I *refused*. It wasn't as if I had anything to hide or to be afraid of, I just didn't see the point of him checking my phone calls. That's like letting somebody read your diary or flip through your private phone book. For what? That's your private shit! I didn't ask to go through *his* phone.

I felt it was all about Travis trying to control me, like a father. But I wasn't looking for a father in him. I didn't need all of that authority shit in my life. I was trying to make my own moves and my own decisions and Travis was trying to be another restriction.

He yelled at me, "Let me see your damn *phone*," and tried to snatch it out of my hands.

I pulled my phone back and said, "No."

Then he got so mad at me that he wrestled the phone from me in the car. Once he had the phone in his hands, he found that he couldn't access it without my code. He got made at that too.

"You fucking dumb bitch!" he screamed at me. Then he threw my phone out his driver side window and jumped out of the car to stomp on it, breaking my phone into pieces. When he was done, he climbed back into the car to drive off as if nothing had happened. He was turning into a fucking *nutcase*.

When I climbed out of his car at my school, I

mumbled to myself, "Fucking lunatic," as I climbed out of the car. I was upset but I didn't want to make a scene at my school. But he damn sure was going to buy me a new phone. And that was only the *start* of Travis getting out of control.

He started following me around in his car and would park sometimes outside of my girlfriend's house from high school and then wait there for hours until I left. I guess he was waiting to see if we would invite young some boys over to see us or something. He was really *pressed* like that, and it was getting on my nerves.

Even when we broke off and on in our relationship, I kept telling him that I wasn't doing anything with anyone and not cheating on him. I was only enjoying myself as a teenager. That didn't mean that I was out there trying to fuck everybody. But no matter how many times I told him, he refused to believe me. Then he would *beg* me to get back with him and tell me that he would change. I even went to my high school's senior prom by myself, because I *surely* wasn't taking Travis or some young guy with me.

Once I graduated from Miami Beach High School, it became much harder for me to live at home with my mom. We started to crash on everything. We were constantly arguing about how long I could stay out, who my friends were, what I wore out to night clubs and definitely about my relationship with Travis. And it wasn't like I planned to stand still either. I immediately enrolled in Dade County Community College to study communications, I found a job working the front desk at a hotel and I started thinking about getting my own place to live.

But after several years of dealing with this much older man, who was obviously pressed to control my tight young, pussy, he pissed me off for good by telling me that he had gotten this other girl pregnant. I guess he wanted to try and hurt me emotionally, but I was already sick and tired of his ass and looking for a way out anyway.

So I told him, "Good. Now you can go back to her and leave me alone then. *Please* leave me alone," I insisted. And he was done as far as I was concerned.

But that wasn't the response from me that Travis wanted. I guess he thought that I was going to break down and cry in a jealous rage or something, but I didn't. I was very happy to finally be rid of him. He had made my young life more complicated that what I needed or wanted.

When I turned nineteen, a few friends hit me up one time to join them out at a night club called Sole On The Ocean on Sunny Isles Beach, and Travis was there. I tried my best to ignore him and go on about my night, but Travis lost it as soon as he saw me out having a good time with my friends. He saw a few guys in the club flirting with me and lost his damn *mind*.

He started walking toward us and yelling, "You stupid bitch! You a *hoe*! You a dumb bitch! You fucking different niggas!" and all of that shit in a jealous rage, hating on me. He had gone insane that night and he was just getting started. And he had like ten guys with him, watching the shit as is it was all fun and games.

I was embarrassed and scared, while trying to escape Travis and his immature rants. At first I ducked inside the ladies room, but he followed me there, still calling me out of my name and embarrassing the hell out of me. I started wishing that my brother Myshion was there to kick his *ass* as that point, but both my brothers were still locked up.

I came out the bathroom and headed to the front door of the club to leave. Obviously, I was no longer enjoying myself. My night out with my girls had turned into a nightmare. Travis had never been that crazy out in public around so many people. We usually had our disputes or whatever in private. So I told my friends that I was leaving and got stepping.

When I got outside the club and rushed over to my

car, a black 1991 Toyota Paseo. I had bought that car with five-hundred dollars that I had saved up from working part time. I worked for a promotional company called Extravaganza, where they hired young people to hold up signs outside in high traffic areas to help promote new businesses, like when Cingular Wireless first came out.

Anyway, when I left the club, I turned and saw that Travis had walked out behind me. So I jumped inside to pull away before he could reach me, and this damn man leaped on top of my car, like a villain in of a horror movie.

"SHIT!" I yelled. I was terrified. I thought he was trying to kill me!

The weight of him jumping on my car like that smashed my front windshield. That's when the girl I went to the club with started talking calling up her boyfriend to come down and kick Travis' ass for fucking up my car like that, while his silly-ass friends all watched it. But I told her not to. I didn't want to drag her and her boyfriend into my issues with this man.

I went straight to the Miami Dade Police Station and they treated it like regular case of a traffic dispute. I thought we could have least pull up a charge and a court case of destruction of property or something. I mean, they could see that the man had fucked up my car. But all the police did was ask me to get my insurance people to fix with it.

I drove my fucked-up car back home and parked it out in front of my mother's house and she went crazy as soon as she saw it. She got me to call Travis up on the phone and she cussed his ass out.

"You tore up my daughter's shit! What's wrong with you?" she hollered at him. She said, "You crazy asshole! Don't you *ever* come around my damn daughter *again*! Do you hear me, you motherfucker?"

My mother was *livid*. She never liked Travis anyway. And I was so fucking *frustrated*. That car only cost me $500 but to fix the windshield would cost me more than that. I wasn't really an accident where I could get my no-fault insurance to fix it. And I didn't have the money to fix it on my own yet, so I let it sit out front for awhile until I finally decided to get rid of it and have it towed away from like a hundred dollars.

Those are the times when a girl really needs her farther and older brothers around for protection. If Pat Pat and Shion were there, it would have never even gotten that far with Travis. My family would have *killed* his ass before he even thought of treating me like that. That's when I *knew* I needed to sever all ties with Travis. He needed to know that he would *never* be getting back with me, so there was no reason for him to even *think* about me anymore.

I reflected back to my first thoughts on Travis and not wanting to call his ass in beginning. My first instincts were never to even deal with him. He wasn't my type and he had never turned me on like that. Nevertheless, I ended up dealing with him for several years, giving him the pussy as much as he wanted it, and he *still* wasn't satisfied until he controlled me like a slave. So I began to feel really depressed with myself and my decision to get involved with this man.

He became so abusive to me physically, sexually and psychologically, that sometimes he even spit in my face when I didn't want to have sex with him. I was so embarrassed and ashamed of myself, but that's what a young girl will allow to happen when her self-esteem and family love is not where it should be.

At that time, my mom had been dating this guy named Jose for about a year, and I didn't particularly care for him. He was a short and thick Spanish guy with this macho demeanor and my mother was very happy with him. But this guy made me *sick* every time I saw him. I was no longer a child and I knew a lot more about life and relationships, and I just didn't like the *vibe* that I got from that man. I had always been into observing people and I could tell that Jose was a womanizer, who liked to give my mother lavish gifts to cover-up his inconsistencies. And I just didn't trust the man.

I tried to warn my mother to watch out for him but she already love struck. I thought my mom could do a lot better than him myself, the same way I knew I could do better than Travis.

Finally, my mom told me, "Dior, we can't have two queens in one house. So you have to *go*."

Well, she couldn't have said it any better, because I had one foot out the door already. By that time, I had my front desk job as a hotel receptionist, making ten dollars an hour and then I got approved for my own apartment for six-hundred dollars a month. It was a tiny, one-bedroom about ten minutes from my mom's house, but it was *mine* and I was proud to be out and on my own.

I remember Travis found out where I lived and drove over to my apartment, trying to kick my front door in. And that was *it*! I called the police to have his ass arrested and got a restraining order to keep his crazy-ass away from me. I could see that I was going to be nothing more than a young bitch to him and there was no love in his heart, only lust, selfishness and anger. And there was no way I was going to allow this man to get used to abusing me and putting his hands on me like so many other women would allow, so I was out of that relationship for *good*.

A few months after I had moved out of the house, I noticed that my mother was always sad and angry. That's when I found out that Jose was married. I don't know if my mom knew that about him earlier, but I assume that she *didn't*, because the next thing I knew, she was in jail for aggravated assault.

My mom had attacked Jose and had been arrested for it. So I went down to the jailhouse to see this barely five-foot-tall woman locked behind bars for assaulting a man who she thought she loved. I had never seen my mother like that before and I felt horrible for her. I couldn't even hug or kiss her and feel her heartbeat against mine. My sisters and I could only sit there and talk to her through a phone and a bullet-proof glass. Once again, I felt devastated. We were both having our problems with crazy-ass men.

By that time, my brother Henry had gotten some girl pregnant and had moved with her and the baby out to Missouri. That's where his girl was originally from, so she wanted her family to help her out with the baby. Well, Henry ended up getting a construction job out there and fixing 4-wheeler motorcycles and stuff. So he wasn't around to help us either. But I was glad that he was doing good for himself.

After being forced to spend time in jail for the assault, my mother moved out of her North Miami house, and she and my baby sister Naomi moved in with me at my tiny little apartment. But my sister Charmaine moved in with my father's people. It's a long story, but they basically liked Weeda better than the rest of us. She was real dark and pretty with smooth skin like my father's people and they were willing to take care of her—rent free and pay her bills—where I had always taken care of myself. So we began to have our difference.

I my sister Charmaine felt some kind of envy about me being older than her and doing my own thing like I did. So my father's family took her in and took care of her. And I stopped calling her Weeda because we were no longer kids. But my sister still liked to call me Dior, particularly when she wanted to bring attention to me doing something that she thought was *extra*.

"I don't know who you think *you* are, *Dior*."

I just had to deal with their perception of me being a diva or whatever. Fuck it. But it was definitely crowded in my tiny one-bedroom apartment. I couldn't bring myself to deny my mother after all that she had done for us and all that she was still going through in her life. I knew how hurt she felt after finding out that Jose was married, so I felt sorry for her.

Since I worked a lot at this hotel, I didn't really recognize how much my mother began to change. I was in and out of the house, while she cooked, cleaned and took care of my two sisters. Then I started to notice that my mother was always looking over her shoulder, behind her back and in the rearview mirror of my car, as if someone was following her. She started acting really paranoid and would barely leave the house.

I thought my mother was going through a phase or something and that she would eventually snap out of it. Obviously, my mother had gone through a lot, but she would always find a way to pull herself together to keep doing what she needed to do in life. But then my mother disappeared for *days* without a word.

My baby sister Naomi was flipping out. "Where's mom? I don't know where mom is. She hasn't come back home."

My mom had been the only parent my baby sister Naomi had, because she still refused to deal with my father after seeing him punch my mother in the face and break her nose years ago. Naomi was fourteen when my mother disappeared like that and she was still very dependent on my mother. She had no idea how to take our mother's absence.

When I finally spoke to my mother, I found that she had broken out to Atlanta, Georgia and was staying up there with relatives. Just from listening to her voice, I could tell that she wasn't coming back to Miami. She was already comfortable there in Atlanta. That's when she admitted that she feared what Jose would do to her from his threats. With him being a Spanish man, she told me

Jose was into the Santa Maria and voodoo shit that had freaked her out and that she didn't want it to extend to her kids. I guess my mom really believed that Jose would try to harm her *and* her family. So she told me that she could never feel comfortable in Miami again.

I didn't really believe in voodoo and family spells like my mother did, but she obviously had been affected by something. All I knew was that I was very upset with my mother for deserted us like that, especially my baby sister Naomi. My mother had basically left the responsibility of raising Naomi to me. But I was only a few years older than her, nineteen to Naomi's fifteen. What did I know about trying to raise a teenager? I was still going through growing pains myself.

Naomi had this idea in her mind from my sister Charmaine that I hadn't been looking out for them. Charmaine had tried to brainwash my sister into feeling like I was only out for myself, which was not true. I was older than them and only trying to live my life as a young woman in Miami and not a little girl. But that didn't mean that I didn't care about them. That was *crazy*. But that's how manipulative Charmaine had become, which was the reason why she decided to stay with our father's family instead of with me.

When I was out at work or doing me as the oldest daughter in the house, my sister would have Naomi out with her, hanging out in our old neighborhood of Overtown until two o'clock in the morning with the wrong crowd of people, during the wrong damn things. I would tell her not to do that shit, but Charmaine would often use that against me by telling Naomi that I thought I was better than them and that I could do whatever I wanted and they couldn't.

Well, *shit*, I had graduated from high school already and was on my way out the house, but Naomi was only a freshman in high school. So I thought that Charmaine should have *known* better than that. Charmaine was only a year younger than me to make her own decisions like that, but Naomi was *five* years younger and still the baby. So once I began to raise her on my own without our mother or family members, Naomi I still had those issues to deal with.

So there I was, stuck trying to provide for myself and for my needy and emotional teenager sister who was still in high school. I thought I was doing a good job of it too. I would break my *neck* to get Naomi anything and everything that she wanted or needed. I would drive her to school every day and make sure she knew that I loved her and had her back, but all I seemed to get in return was defiance and back talk whenever she decided to act out.

"You're not my mother. You can't tell me what to do."

I said, "As long as you're living in my *house* and I'm paying all the fucking *bills*, I can."

Naomi wanted to keep hanging out late and running around in the streets with Charmaine and not go to school and I wasn't going to *allow* that shit.

It was to the point where I thought daily about throwing her ass out and letting her see how hard it would be without me *for real*. I was working overtime hours and everything to provide for my sister. But then I would think about my mom and want to finish the job that she had not finished. I couldn't bring myself to abandon Naomi like our mother had. However, she was *really* fucking trying me.

One time, it got so bad that we had a fist fight out in the street in front of my car. I was nearly ready to *kill* my sister that day. I had gotten a call from her school and they told that she hadn't been showing up for her classes. So I drove up there to see the principal and teachers and she's not at school. I got so mad that I hunted her ass down at my aunt's house to confront her about it and she started disrespecting me right out in the middle of the street.

"You not gonna tell me what to do, *Dior*," and all of that shit. By that time, Naomi was a big-ass girl; light complexioned like Myshion and nearly six feet tall with a big body. She wasn't small like my sister Charmaine was. So Naomi figured she could put her hands on me. That's when I lost it and we started fighting right beside my car.

I was like, "Are you motherfucking *crazy*?!" I was so *mad*.

Can you imagine breaking your *ass* for somebody and they keep telling you what they're *not* going to do and how you can't tell them anything? It wasn't as if I was trying to be extra strict on her. But if I ask you to do what you're supposed to do in school and be in the house at a certain time—while you're still a young teenager who can get in all kinds of trouble out in the streets—then I didn't see anything *wrong* with that. It's what any big sister or parent would do. And at that point, that's what I was, my little sister's *guardian*, whether she liked it or not. I couldn't have her running around out in the streets, doing whatever the hell she wanted. Every day I was worried *sick* about my sister and hoping that she was safe and making good decisions. So you can only *imagine* how much stress was on me at nineteen. But I had to keep it moving. I had nobody to depend on but myself.

As time passed by, I started working nearly eighty hours a week to keep my bills paid and baby sister fed, clothed and her hair done. I was doing everything I could to make sure that my sister had everything that she needed. I even cut back on my own needs and expenses for her, while driving a broken down-ass, 1998 blue Buick Oldsmobile and everyday there was something else going wrong with that damn car. But I kept getting it fixed until I finally gave up on it.

One day, while heading into work, that car finally broke down on me for good. So I started having to take the bus until I could get another car. I remember I waited at the bus stop for *two hours* one night and the bus never game. So I had to walk my behind home. Another time—with me not being familiar with the bus routes—I got off the bus at the wrong stop and ended up having to walk the rest of the way home after three o'clock in the morning with tears running down my face. Man, I was going through it. But I kept going.

I couldn't believe my bad luck sometimes. I was busting my ass to stay above water for me and my baby sister, but it seemed like everything was going wrong. I thought again about Louis coming back into my life to help me through it, but he was long gone. I even thought about calling Travis crazy-ass back up to help me out. That's just how desperate I was. But I had made a promise to *God* that I would never go back to that man. I just couldn't allow myself to tolerate a man trying to abuse me like he had. So I still refused to call him.

By the time I got home that night, it was four AM in the morning and my feet were killing me. I kicked my shoes off, while still wearing my work uniform and fell asleep right there on the living-room sofa. Obviously, I had my hands full. I was just a young girl trying to do right in a grown-up world.

I don't know if it was just by coincidence, but around that same time that I was going through those struggles with no car, I found an advertisement for a strip club near Naomi's book bag. It was crazy, because I usually didn't check through her things like that, but this cut out piece of paper just fell out on the floor, as if Naomi had stuffed it in her bag at the last minute without really thinking about it. She was older by then, like fifteen or sixteen, but she was still in high school.

I looked at this advertisement for a strip club and was pissed that my sister was even looking at some shit like that. So I confronted sister about it.

I held the paper up in front of her said, "Naomi,

45

where did you get this? Don't bring this shit into my house."

But she stood up there and she denied everything. She said, "What's that? I don't know what that is. I don't even know where they came from."

I was getting the experience of a parent *early*, because I knew *damn well* that I didn't bring that shit up into my house myself. And I had found it was right next to my sister's book bag. That's sounds obviously *guilty* to me, right?

To make a long story short, Naomi promised that she would never do it again and I didn't see, hear or think anything else about it. But then Naomi started living at my Aunt Tasha's house, my mother's baby sister. My mother had heard rumors about having brothers and sisters, who were all split up and sent in different places as kids, so they all started to find out about each other as adults. My mother even had a *twin* who was separated from her. That's all a whole other book to write. But that's just how broken and crazy my family was. I mean, it is what it is.

So anyway, my Aunt Tasha had five children of her own and lived in South Miami and Naomi knew that she could get away with whatever she wanted over there. She had it all planned out to act a fool. But I couldn't force my sister to stay with me. And to tell the truth, I was able to find some peace of mind without her there.

Without having to worry about Naomi every day, I felt a huge relief of the constant pressure that I was under. And when I finally had a day off from work without her, I couldn't *believe* how relaxing it was. I call a phone call that same Sunday night from my long-time girlfriend Precious to hang out. I had known Precious since back and grade school, so I decided to hang out with her and few of my other girls that night.

First we went to this spot downtown called Club Nocturnal, where the Atlanta-based rapped Young Jeezy was performing. His first album was off the chain and his music and swagger was killing it out in the streets *and* on the radio, so I was excited to go. I got to see Young Jeezy perform live in Miami and Club Nocturnal was in a downtown area, where you felt safe from robberies and violence. And dozens of dope boys came out that night to show off their cars, jewelry money.

At the time, I was dressed casual but still sexy with black jeans and a black blazer that had ruffles at the bottom. I was feeling confident and good that night, like a young woman should. I was legal too at twenty-one years old, and the club was *insane* that Sunday night. It was the place to be!

After we left the Club Nocturnal and the Young Jeezy performance, Precious wasn't ready to head home yet. She was still feeling riled up and adventurous, so I went with her and her girls as they pulled up to a strip club called CoCo's in an area that we called Lake Side, near North Miami. But I still wasn't too fond of strip clubs and I heard a lot of craziness about them, so I wasn't going up in there.

I told my girl Precious, "You know what? I'll wait for y'all out in the car."

I had no idea how long they planned to be in there, but I didn't want to go and would not have felt bad if they had all changed their minds either. I had never been to strip club before and I wasn't at all interested, especially after finding that shit in my sister's book bag about them. But Precious started begging me.

"What? Girl, you can't sit out here in the damn car. Come on in with us. It's only dancing. Come on."

I shook my head and said, "That ain't the kind of dancing I want to see."

Precious said, "Aw, girl, stop acting like that. We *grown* now, we ain't in grade school no more. Get off that stuck-up shit and enjoy yourself. Come on, girl, please.

Why you don't want to hang out with us?"

Precious remembered when my mom was strict on me and how I always kept my nose out of the streets and more into my books and work. However, Precious had been raised around a lot of boys, who had taken her around strip clubs and stuff where I hadn't been. So she kept pleading with me to go until I finally agreed to it.

When we walked in, I wasn't impressed with this place at all. I guess I expected much more from the way people talked about strip clubs and wanted to go there. But it just looked like a cheap, dark club to me. It was crowded in that place on Saturday night but I didn't recognize anyone that was in there.

Precious and her girls were getting all into, but I all I did was set back and watch. I observed who all of the girls were, the guys who were spending big money on them and how these girls were dressed and dancing. And since I had never been in a strip club before or even thought about it, I was turned out at how a pretty face and a fat ass had enticed all these money-getting niggas to spend their hard-earned cash on these bitches.

Like I said, I was busting my ass for eighty hours a week on ten dollars an hour, while these strip club bitches were getting hundreds of dollars right there in front on me, when I had only been up in the club for a few minutes. I don't know what Precious and her girls were thinking, but all I could think about was the money. I couldn't get that shot off my mind. I *needed* money like that.

So I immediately started imagining if I had the confidence to take my ass out there and dance for money. Just like that, the money had turned me out, and I didn't even want to go in that place at first. But it's not like I was ready to take my damn clothes off that *week* and start dancing for dollars. I was only *thinking* about it.

With more time to myself on my hands, without

having to care for my baby sister anymore, I began to feel lonely for a man again. So after five year without him, I became so pressed to find Louis and pull him back into my life that I asked this guy named Burrado from the old neighborhood if he knew him. Everyone called him Rado for short. He was trying to talk to me himself, but I was feeling him like that. I told him if he wanted to make some money, all he had to do was find Louis for me and I would give him a hundred dollars. That's how desperate I was.

He was like, "Louis? You mean LT. That's my *man*. All right, I can do that."

Everyone called Louis "LT" and it took Rado only day before he called me back up. At first I thought Rado was bullshitting me. I had been looking for Louis for *years* and cold never find him, but then Rado found him in just *one* damn day? I couldn't believe it, but then he put Louis on the phone.

Louis said, "Oh my God, this is my girl. What's going on?" He was shocked to hear from me too. He thought that he would have to hunt me down. He was like, "Did you miss me?"

Once I heard his voice, I was excited as hell. I knew Louis' voice from anywhere and I loved him dearly. I said, "Of *course*, I missed you. I missed you like crazy. Where are you?"

He said, "I'm at Rado's house."

I said, "I'm coming there right now."

Louis told me that he had been picked by the Feds the next day after hanging out with me and they had sentenced him to five years. That explained his sudden disappearance. I knew something was wrong with how he disappeared like that, but I didn't have enough information at that time to find out more about it. Louis told me he didn't want to break my heart by telling me and he didn't want me to wait for him while he was in jail, so he didn't want to tell me anything.

Well, I didn't waste no time. I even borrowed a car to drive and see him in North Miami. Rado was there when I pulled up and was hounded me about that hundred dollars, even though I found out that he and Louis were homeboys. But I gave him the money anyway. I guess that was the easiest one-hundred dollars that he had ever made.

I greeted Louis and kissed his scared face as soon as I saw him. He had picked up a little muscle weight in jail, but he still looked pretty much the same with a fresh haircut. I was happy to see him and I wanted to fuck him instantly. Louis was the only guy that I thought I could have sex with who wouldn't try to hurt me. And even though we had never had sex before, I still considered him my first love. So I wanted to show him what he had missed and what I had been saving up for him.

As a grown woman with regrets or confusions about my love for him, I drove Louis right back to my apartment and fucked him something *fierce*. It was a sex fiesta inside my apartment. We fucked all over my apartment; on the bed, the floor, the sofa, the kitchen and even over bathroom sink. I wanted to give Louis my all and let him see how much I missed him. Words couldn't even begin to explain it.

Since I knew that Louis was just getting out of jail and trying to get back on his feet, I was willing to give him anything he needed to get by; food, clothes, money or whatever. If I was in the same situation and needed something from him, I had no doubt that he would have done the same by looking out for me.

After a few more months back out on the streets, Louis started to get money again. I couldn't expect for him to keep taking charity from a woman, and it wasn't like I could give him *big* money. Louis was twenty-five years old, so he wanted to get his own cake and I couldn't even complain about that. He was a grown-ass man. But once he started getting money, I couldn't see that it wasn't about me and him anymore. He started to change and pull away from me. He had his own ideas about what he wanted to do and how he wanted to spend it.

And you know what? I wasn't even mad at him. Louis was still my heart and it was fun while it lasted. But I continued to see that I couldn't count on *anyway*. It was a dog eat dog world out there and everybody cared more about themselves than anyone else. So I started thinking more and more about taking care of *me*.

Sometime after that, I got a call from my girlfriend Terri, who told me she saw my baby sister Naomi dancing in this strip club in South Miami.

I was like, "*What?* No you *didn't?* What club are you talking about?"

At first, I didn't believe her. Naomi was only sixteen at the time and I couldn't believe that she would go ahead and do some shit like that after I had talked to her about a year ago. So I drove my raggedy-ass Buick down there after getting it fixed and hoping that it wouldn't break down on me again.

I pulled up to this club in South Miami called The Playpen, and that shit was jam *packed*. I was dressed down in an all black hoody and pants that night so I could blend in with the dark crowd instead of standing out. I was there for one reason and one reason only, and that was to see if my sister was up in there and to drag her ass back out if she was.

I pushed, shoved and stepped my way through this crowded-ass strip club, trying to find my baby sister, while bumping into people and stepping on a few people's toes. That's how pissed and reckless I was that night. I was dam near ready to fight anybody who had something to say to me. But when I couldn't find my sister, I took a deep breath and felt relief. I was then ready to leave. I felt that it was all a false alarm and I could breathe normally again. But as I headed back toward the front door, I finally spotted my sister on a stage.

Once I saw her dancing onstage, I was in *shock*. My baby sister was a beautiful and very intelligent girl and I just couldn't imagine her like that, but it was definitely *real*. The DJ even had a name for her; he called her Conceited, as if she *knew* she was the shit.

Naomi was wearing a one-piece top that covered her breast and her private parts like a thong, while the back of it exposed *all* of her young ass with red, three-inch heels. I couldn't believe what I was witnessing. Strip club dancing was *definitely* not the life that I had envisioned for her. And after all of my strutting around at the strip club—while thinking that I would do something crazy that night—I watched as all of these guys threw money on my sister and I couldn't take it. All I could imagine was the big scene that she would make if I walked up there and snatched her off that stage, while all of those lustful niggas with big money paid to watch her dance for them.

So I did the only thing I thought would be sane; I walked the hell out of there without my sister ever seeing me, and I didn't look back. I figured I would deal with her ass as soon as I got her away from there alone again. And I was sure that my sister Charmaine already knew about it. Knowing her, she had probably encouraged Naomi to do that shit in the first place.

I was still conflicted about my baby sister's decision to get money at such a young and innocent age at the strip club, but I can't even lie, I started to think about my own job and how little money I was making. You were always walking on eggshells at these jobs, knowing that the white managers and owners could fire you at anytime for whatever made-up reason, like they done with other black and Spanish workers. So I never really felt secure on my job.

Sure enough, they started writing me up for different reasons and giving me warnings on the job for coming late and stuff. You had to deal with the pressure and the fear of being fired everyday because you had no other choice. Realistically, I no longer liked that hotel job anymore because it didn't pay me enough for all of the hours I worked there. So once I had an option, my fear of being fired was no longer there. I had a new way of making faster, easier and bigger money now.

Then I got a call from my from another childhood friend named Vicky. I told her all about the problems that I was having on my job, and Vicky said that she was having money problems of her own. We were both in the same boat, two young and beautiful women, who were both caught up in the rat race of life. I even stopped attending Dade County Community College. With all that I had going on, I couldn't go to school and still provide for myself on my own. I had to *work* to live and I just didn't have enough time or focus to do it all.

So Vicky started talking about this other strip club in South Miami, right near the club where I found my sister dancing. And it all came down to me making a money decision. Either I could keep looking for a better job with no education and no money to get an education—while still needing money to live. Or I could wait around for some uncountable guy to take care of me, which I couldn't see happening, because everybody was out for themselves.

I wish I could tell you a *Cinderella* story, where I lose a damn shoe and some rich prince finds it and comes searching to find me and save my ass. But this was real life in Miami, Florida, and I was a poor black girl with broken-ass family who found herself all on her own and running out of options. So I thought to myself *Fuck it! Let me just make this money and to hell with everything else.*

I told my girl Vicky, "All right, let's go. Let's do it." It was all about the money for me. But deep down inside, I was nervous as hell and I felt like a big hypocrite. However, I would rather be a hypocrite with some money in my pocket than walking around *broke*, dignified and homeless. Oh, fuck that! So you can judge me if you want, but I decided that my life was about to change … for better or for worse.

I Can Do That

Before Vicky and I walked into this South Miami strip club, I couldn't even think straight and was ready to back out of it. But Vicky was all excited and I didn't want to disappoint her by changing my mind at the last minute. So I went through with it and walked up into this small strip club prepared to dance. I figured if my little sister could do it, then I could do it even *better* and make *more* money.

As soon as we walked in, we saw that Trick Daddy was up in the club that night with a lot of competition for us. But it was too late for us to care at that point. We had made up our minds to take our clothes off and get that money. We approached the club manger about dancing and he immediately asked us about paying a bar fee.

I was like "What? We have to pay to dance?" We didn't know what he was talking about. It wasn't like we had stripped at a club before, so how would we know about that? It was all new to me.

He said, "Yeah, all dancers have to pay a bar fee to work here."

I asked him how much that was, and he said forty dollars. But sometimes they could charge you more than that, depending on what night it was and how crowed it was. Like on a holiday weekend, they would try to charge you up to three-hundred dollars.

When he asked me what I wanted to call myself. I shrugged and said, "Dior." I damn sure wasn't going to tell him Keisha. I didn't want those people in there to know me like that. And as far as I was concerned, I was only experimenting. Dancers all made up names for themselves anyway. And Dior fit me. It was simple and to the point, and my mom *definitely* would have called my ass Dior for deciding to strip. But I didn't plan to tell anyone about it.

Anyway, this club wasn't big at all. Only about a hundred to a hundred-fifty people were in there. It was dirty and raggedy too. I guess Trick Daddy wanted to be incognito in a small and grimy place like that. Me and Vicky were doing the same thing. We didn't want to start out a club where everybody knew us, just in case we didn't like it. But once everyone sees you, it would be too late to go back.

Well, the manager realized that we were new girls who didn't know the game yet, so he let us dance without our fee, but we would have to pay it at the end of the night before we left. He didn't ask us anything else, didn't give us any rules, a pep talk, guidance or none of that shit. It was all up to us to do what we do and learn on the fly.

And let me tell you, as soon as the other girl's in the club found out that we were there to danced and get money, this one dancer with a Princess tattoo across her booty tried to pick a fight with us.

She said, "You new hoes bet' not touch my shit."

This bitch was raggedy just like the club. If I was a guy, I wouldn't have touched her with a ten-foot pole. She looked like she needed to retire. She was short and dark with a little bit of an ass but with no attractiveness or sex appeal. She had a flat chest like a teenage boy and looked dirty like a street trick on drugs. I'm not exaggerating either. But that type of bickering between dancers was all a part of the strip club game. Every time new girls would walk up in the club, the old bitches would get jealous. But this Princess girl was no competition for us *at all*. So Vicky and I went inside the back room to get dressed in our costumes to dance without even thinking about her ass.

We hit the dance floor that first night, thinking strictly about the money. I didn't care about any of the other girls in there. That wasn't my job. My job was to entertain the customers with my nice ass, my titties and seductive movements. And that's just what I did. But as soon as I hit the floor, one young guy grabbed my hip and instructed me to dance on him.

I danced for about two minutes before this guy pushed me off of him. I was shocked and embarrassed by it. I didn't know what I was doing wrong. He didn't pay me anything either.

His thuggish homeboy was smiling right beside him. He grabbed me by my hand and pulled me over to him to whisper in my ear through the music and asked me to dance for him.

That's the strip club business for you. You go from dancing for one guy to the next. So I danced for his friend in my clear, high-heeled boots and brown panty and bra set until my feet were sore. I didn't even know what I was doing, but was just moving ass around.

When I was finished dancing, this guy pressed three-hundred dollars in my hand with his phone number written down on a piece of paper. I guess he must have already had it written out or something, because he damn sure didn't write it down while I was dancing. That was another part of the strip club business; guys were constantly trying to get with you outside the club. But I wasn't thinking about his phone number; I was thinking about the three-hundred dollars that he had given me just for shaking my ass on him.

I couldn't *believe it*! It took me a whole *week* to make that much money on my job. Just like that, I was hooked. And it was a Tuesday or Wednesday night or a weekday. So I planned to call my job and let them know that I would be calling off work the next day, so I could get some more of that fast strip club money. However, the manager wasn't trying to hear it.

I told him, "Mario, I won't be able to make it in tomorrow, I have a family emergency."

Mario said, "Well, it's too late. No one is gonna come in to fill your shift now on the schedule."

I knew that he was telling the truth. I had waited too long to call him with my excuse and Mario was only doing his job. But fuck it, I wasn't going back in.

I said, "Well, I have an emergency. What else do you want me to tell you?"

"I don't know," he grumbled over the phone.

All I knew was I didn't plan to be locked into that job anymore, so I decided to tell him to use that as my two-week notice so I could quit and move on.

That's how serious I was about getting that money. That hotel job wasn't paying me *half* the money that I could make in just a few nights at the strip clubs. So next step up was Club Angels, what everyone called "The A." It was back up in North Miami, where Vicky and I knew people. That raggedy-ass club in South Miami had given us the confidence that we needed to take the next step.

Actually, The A wasn't that much better than the first club. It was still raggedy and held only two-hundred people. And the dressing room was tiny. But it was a more familiar area for us. It was closer to where we lived and we both knew that it was more money there. So I expected to *kill it* back home in North Miami and the Beach. I already knew all of the money niggas in the area, who went to the strip club from the streets or from high school. And I knew that they would look out for me because they were always attracted to me.

As for my girl Vicky, I found out that she couldn't really take the strip club crowd. The atmosphere was too much for her so she would start drinking and shit. And once she started drink to get herself in the mood, she would overdo it and lose her focus. She didn't really know how to work the club on the business level like I did. To be honest, she was starting to worry me and get in my fucking way. I didn't want to be out there *babysitting* her. So I stopped calling her ass to go with me.

Vicky didn't really didn't have that go-get-girl attitude like I had anyway. She didn't feel like making money the way I did. She would complain about not having it, but then she didn't have the work ethic to go get it. She was a very pretty girl and all that, but she just wasn't cut out for hard work. So she moved in to live with her family members and freeloaded on them like my little sisters would do with our family. But I never did that shit *once*. I was used to getting my own and I was prepared to keep doing it too.

Even though I called myself Dior in the strip club, I had dozens of guys from my old high school and the North Miami neighborhood who recognized me. Dior had only been my family name so it wasn't like people out in the streets had called me that. But a lot of these guys wanted to hook up with me before as Keisha and I hadn't paid them any mind. Now they had a chance to pay me to dance for them as Dior. And they jumped at the opportunity.

As soon as I started dancing at The A the guys were like, "Hey, ain't your name Keisha? Don't I know you?"

I smiled and said, "Yeah, you know me, but it's *Dior* now."

I didn't want them calling me Keisha in there. I had to make a clear separation between the two. And Dior it was all about the money, so there was no need in even knowing me as Keisha. I wasn't giving up any free dances because we went to high school together. I was all professional in there and I *needed* to be, because there were a lot of reject girls there trying to do just about *anything* for forty dollars. I didn't want to be mixed up with them. A lot of these girls had lived some hard-ass lives and had all

59

kinds of issues that they needed to work out. But I was a fresh face with a fresh perspective on getting mine and keeping away from all the other bullshit.

For instance, I learned real fast not to dance anywhere near the DJ booth. This club was really dark in that area—nearly pitch black—where the older guys were bold enough to pull their dicks out. They expected more than just dancing, but I wasn't going for it. I let everybody in that club know that *Dior* played strictly by the get-money rules or nothing. So, if you weren't talking money to me, I wasn't trying to hear you. And the guys respected me for that and looked out for me with big paper in there. That's how you have to be if you want to make it in the strip club. You have to let them know that you're no easy dummy. But since a lot of the guys in North Miami already knew me from my no-time-for-boys days, they already knew what time it was, making my job to get money from dancing much easier. They didn't have rules and shit at The A either, so I just showed up and did my own thing.

I was able to make some good money there too, from $1,200 to $1,500 a night sometimes. But a lot of people who weren't from that area didn't like to go up in The A, so it was harder to make more than the normal crowd there had to give, you know. Even the people who lived in the area were scared to go there some nights because of the shootings, robberies and fights that would go on.

It took no time at all before Louis showed up one night and asked me what I was doing there.

I was like, "Hello, I'm getting money." The shit was obvious. Why else would I be in there?

After Louis and I had parted ways and stopped dating, I didn't really pay him any mind anymore. I wasn't hating on him. There was no beef between us, I just didn't have the time or energy for a guy who no longer had the time for me, especially if he wasn't going look out for me the way I had done for him. So how dare he step up and try to tell me how to get mine? There was no sense in us ever being *friends*, for real. I didn't have the same respect for Louis.

He tried to grab my arm and pull me over to the bar, but I wasn't really trying to go with him.

He said, "Well, if you trying to get money like that, you need to dance at Take One."

I broke away from him and we went our separate ways, but I did think about what he told me. Once I jumped into the strip club business, I heard about a lot of different clubs. I had no reason to know about them before I got into the business.

I had heard the The Uno had a whole lot of celebrities, who would show up there, you know, big money hustlers, rappers and athletes. But I didn't think much about dancing there. I was just getting my feet wet and still learning what I needed to do. I didn't know how to climb and slide down a pole yet, I didn't know how to twerk and I didn't even really know how to dance. I was just sticking my ass out and bending over with a nice shape and pretty-ass face and hair. And new girls always got play. The club wasn't that much competition. They had a pole with bitches who knew how to work it but it still wasn't anything special.

I dropped all of my guilt trips about strip dancing and continued to do what I had to do to make money. I didn't even talk to my baby sister Naomi about it. I just understand that she had to survive like everyone else, so I could no longer ride her anymore, especially while *I* was stripping. How could I say anything? It would have been hypocritical.

After awhile, I was doing all right. It was much better than standing on my feet behind a desk all day for a measly pay check that I had to wait two weeks for. I was making hundreds of dollars a *night* and *thousands* a week sometimes. I was paying all of my bills, buying myself new clothes, boots and outfits, and I had extra money to spend on myself and my family. I even bought a new car, a red Ford Focus that I didn't have to worry about breaking down on me.

Before I knew it, I had quickly fallen in love with dancing, mainly because it was so easy, particularly if you had a pretty face or a nice body. If you had both, it was double trouble and *triple* trouble if you had and finesse with it. It's all about knowing how to be smooth and talk to a nigga real good. That's when you really get the money.

"Damn, you smell really good tonight. How was your day at work? You deserve nothing bit the best."

You know, you have to tell them anything they want to hear and make them *believe it.*

I had ended my two-year run as a front-desk attendant at the hotel I worked at to start a more lucrative career in strip dancing, and I was no longer apologetic about it. You basically had to pick your way to live and live it. It wasn't like I was committing a crime or anything. I wasn't fucking anybody for money and it was my body to dance with as a grown-ass woman.

Speaking of being a grown-ass woman, my baby sister Naomi was *not*. So she ended up moving back in with me at my one-bedroom apartment, where she slept in my room, while I slept on the sofa. She was seventeen-years old and could still learn a lot from an older sister. That's not to say that I was perfect or anything, but I had been out there on my own way longer and had made a lot more decisions on my own than either one of my sisters. I was still the oldest, the first one to work and the first to be out of the house with my own shit. So no one in my family could really argue about me taking care of myself. I never moved in with *anyone*; not even with a guy. They wanted me to love in for my damn money but I was like "No thank you."

After my sister Naomi had moved back in with me, I took her to the doctor's office at the OBGYN to get a routine check up and the doctor called us back in to talk about it. I had dreamt that Naomi was pregnant, but didn't say anything to her about it. I didn't want it to be true. But during the time that she wasn't living with me, I had no idea what she had been doing or *if* she had been protecting herself. I never even asked her why she came back, I was just glad she was back where I can watch over her. And we had a good, long talk about the strip club

I basically told my sister that I was *embarrassed* when I saw her stripping down in South Miami. I mean, she was still in fucking *high school!*

Naomi said, "Well, what do you *expect*, Keisha. Our mom walked out on us. I don't even talk to our fucking dad. I just got tired of having to depend on people to take care of me."

I said, "Yeah, but that's what *I'm* here for, Naomi, to make sure your okay. I don't want you out there in the streets with that shit. You need to be in school, finishing your education and preparing for your future."

When we got back to the doctor's office that day, they confirmed that my baby sister was three months pregnant. I immediately told her that I didn't think that she should have a baby at that age and with no way to provide for it. Naomi was still a teenager with no high school diploma and no job to support herself and the baby, because she surely couldn't dance while pregnant. She didn't even have a place to live. I didn't even know if the baby's father was ready for all of that, but Naomi was adamant about having the baby anyway.

"No, Keisha, I want my baby. I'm not having no abortion."

What could I do? I couldn't *force* her to do it. It was her body and her baby. But yet, I was the one who had to work to provide for her. Then my older brother Myshion was released from prison after being away for eight years. He didn't have anywhere to go so I took him in. My brother didn't have a job, money, food, clothes, shoes or even socks and underwear. On top of that, my sister Charmaine came back to live with me.

Charmaine had moved in with this old-ass guy in is forties and was living with him until they got into their finale argument and she decided to move out. And when they broke up—with her not having any other place to go—my sister ended up moving in with me, even though she didn't really like me like that anymore.

So there I was again, with three of my family members living with me at my small-ass, one-bedroom apartment, and I had to provide for *everything*. That was the family I was born into and there was no running away from them, so I went back to work at the strip club and dealt it with it.

I even asked around and made a few phone calls to get my brother lined up for a construction job. You can't have a grown-ass man back out on the street from prison with no job. That was a sure recipe for disaster. But Myshion didn't even call this man back about the job and ended up right back in jail with me having to pay more money to bail his ass out.

Then my brother had the *nerve* to get upset at me because I didn't want to give him money to start shit back up out in the streets.

He yelled in my face, "You don't give a *fuck* about me!" because I *refused* to give him the money. And you know what he wanted to do with it; *hustle*. But I wasn't having it. Not with *my* hard-earned money. And I did give a *damn* that he was mad about it. He should have taken that construction job I had lined up for him. But he said it wasn't enough money for him.

Maybe not, but at least it would have kept his ass out of jail or the graveyard. But my brother wasn't thinking about that. Myshion only knew one way to live, and that was out on the damn *streets*. So I knew that no matter how much I tried to help him, it was never going to work out. My brother would never be satisfied.

All of that extra stress from my family living with me again pushed me over the limit. I couldn't take it anymore. I needed my own space a breath of fresh air again. So when the rental company started stressing me over an unpaid light bill for something as small as *sixty dollars*, I knew it was finally time for me to go. I had been in that one place for far too long. I then told them that I would not being renewing my lease. Then I would see what my family members would do without a place to stay.

Another one of my childhood friends from school named Von had an older sister Ebony, who was looking for a roommate to help pay for a two-bedroom apartment. So I packed up my shit and moved in with her, giving me an excuse not to deal with my family anymore. But I couldn't leave Naomi hanging, while she was still pregnant. So I moved my baby sister into her first apartment of her own, where she could do what she wanted and learn how to look after herself. Of course, I still had to help her pay for the rent, but at least she would get to see what living on your own as adult was about. I thought the experience would help teach her a few things before she had the baby. I bought her new furniture for her place and everything.

Meanwhile, Charmaine moved back in with our father's people and Myshion ended up moving out to Missouri with Henry and his family. At first I thought it was a crazy-ass idea. I felt for sure that Myshion would get himself into some kind of trouble out there and come right back home to Florida. But it never happened. Henry hooked him up with a job for the same construction company where he worked and Shion fell right in line. I guess he just needed a change of atmosphere and to get away from Miami.

I continued working at Club Angels, but things started to get crazy there and it was no longer safe. I kept going there anyway to get that money until there was a shoot-out inside the club one night. I didn't even know how they got the guns in there past the security. The DJ called my name to report to front stage, and as I got ready to go up, gunshots rang out.

BOOM!

POP! POP! POP!

I was on my way up the steps to the stage and nearly fell flat on my face, trying to run back down from it. I ended ducking into a back room behind that stage, where another stripper and the club manager had ran to hide. None of us knew what the hell was going on out there, but knew we didn't want to be shot at, so we remained in hiding.

Once the gunshots stopped, I snuck out to the back of the club and saw one of the security officers laying face down in a puddle of blood. I stooped down beside him and sat on the floor, panicking. I didn't know what to do but I had to do *something*. He was looking up at me and wheezing for his life.

I held his head in my lap and told him, "You're gonna make it. You're gonna make it."

I was trying to stay positive, hoping that someone would come and help him. But all he talked about was his mother and how hurt she would be.

He said, "My mom just lost my brother last week. What is she gonna do now?"

Finally someone found us and moved me away, while carrying him toward the front of the club to wait for an ambulance to come. Man, I couldn't believe that happened right in front of me. Being that close to death had only happened in the movies. Of course, I knew people who had died out in the streets of Miami before. But I had never been that close to actually *touch* someone

66

who had been shot like that. It was an unreal experience.

The next day, I found out from the club manager that the security officer had died from his gunshot wounds. That forced me to think again about club Uno, where Louis told me the real money was. I wasn't about to stop stripping, but I didn't want to lose my damn life in a raggedy-ass club for money either. So I had to give some serious thought about moving on up to the next level again. And after that shoot out, where I touch a man on his last breath, I made a promise to myself that I would never step foot in The A again. It was time for my ass to move on.

Dior's World

Before I even thought about stripping, I would sometimes drive by this club called The Uno on the west side of Miami in Little Haiti. The Uno always had expensive luxury cars that were parked outside—Bentleys, Porsches, Maybach Benzes, Lamborghinis, Cadillac SUVs, you name it. They were the kind of cars that I would only see on TV commercial, but I never thought that I would ever *own* one of them. They were more like my *dream* cars. So I thought nothing of it. I looked at those cars as unattainable.

But this club Uno was always packed with top-notch dancers. So the name we called it fit. It was the one strip club where everybody wanted to be, or at least the black people of Miami. White people had their own strip clubs, mostly in Miami Gardens.

I had heard a lot about the young dimes and old madams who danced at Uno, as well as the hustlers and big money ball players who hung out and spent money there. I can't say that I was all that intimidated by it, I just didn't have enough confidence to go in there. So I had to talk myself into it. And there was no Vicky or anyone else to help me do it—it was just me.

I kept telling myself that Louis believed in me. He believed I was fine enough to compete. Even though we were not together like that anymore, he still felt that I had what it took. And once Louis starting getting money out on the streets, he knew where *all* of the hot spots were around Miami. So I didn't doubt it. I just needed to do that shit like Nike. It was Dior's *world!* So I pumped myself up not to be afraid of *anything*.

When I finally got up the nerve to do it, I decided to go during the dayshift. It's harder to get in on the night shift at a new club where you haven't proved yourself yet. So I just wanted to get my feet wet. And it was on a Monday morning when I walked in to see if I could make some money there.

Once I reached the door of the club with the bouncers, I became a nervous wreck. I couldn't help myself. It was all anxiety I guess, because I heard so much about this place and expected so much. But the first thing I noticed when I walked in was the low capacity of the club.

I thought, *What the hell was all the fuss about?*

According to the fire code sign on the wall, this place could only hold a hundred-fifty people. I was expecting something *big* since people were talking so much about it. The Uno was no bigger than the rest of strips clubs that I had been to. However, the décor was definitely nicer. They had designed the club with flashy lights that made the place glow like a Christmas tree.

Then I noticed that they had a juke box that played all of the music with no DJ in sight. I thought that was odd. DJs usually gave the clubs a live feel to them. But they told me that the DJ came in after six o'clock to get ready for the night shift.

I walked over to the bar to talk business and was greeted by the day manager. She was a thick high yellow woman, who looked just like Miss Piggy from *The Muppets*. I asked her a few questions about dancing there at the club and I could tell that she was checking me out, while I spoke to her. But she said I had to wait until the club's general manager Big Pete saw me to be hired.

"Pete does all of the hiring himself. So you'll have to talk to him before you do anything." But she told me he was scheduled to be there soon.

I nodded to her and chilled, ready to wait the process out. "Okay."

I heard a lot about Pete too. I even saw him on the *First 48* TV show, where they talked about all of the murders, robberies and crime in the Miami area. They had a story about the original owner of The Uno was killed in a robbery. He was a white man who had owned the club for a long time before these guys tried to stick up the club and found him in there and ended up shooting him. So Big Pete basically ended up running the whole club himself, because the owner's wife didn't really bother with it.

Pete was a big, chocolate brown and muscular man, who was well over six feet and built like a football player. People said that he used to play ball before and he still looked like he could smash into people. He had this physical intimidation and street toughness about him. He was the kind of hard-edged guy who you wouldn't want to fuck him.

After waiting around at the bar for him to arrive, Miss Piggy told me to be patient and that Pete would be there shortly. After another fifteen minutes or so, he walked through the door on a mission and went straight to his office. He didn't even bother to speak to anyone.

I was like, *Shit! Is that how he acts?* I started getting nervous again. Pete didn't seem like a friendly manager at all. Miss Piggy then walked out from the bar and followed right behind him to his office.

I continued to wait there at the barstool for the next move when Miss Piggy walked out and signaled for me to follow her back into Pete's office. So I stood up and followed her lead. As soon as I walked in, Pete asked to see my ID before he told me to fill out a bunch of paperwork for application.

I was like, *What the fuck? Dancers have to fill out paperwork too?*

On top of that, it was more paperwork than I had ever filled out for a regular *job*. I wasn't used to all that shit ad it was annoying. But Uno ran a tight-ass operation and they were not willing to let any underage girls slip in, like my sister. So they had you to sign a bunch of paperwork to cover their asses.

Pete then told me to stand up and to show me the goods. "Lift your dress up and pull your panties down. Let me see what you're working with."

I stood up and did what he told me and exposed my body to him. I felt like a cow at the meat market, but that was the nature of the business. He had to check me out.

Pete nodded and said, "Your breasts are tiny, your stomach is flat, you got a nice fat ass and a pretty pussy. But you need to trim up your pussy hairs a little bit." Then he told me to pull my dress back down. "So, when are you coming back in to work for us?"

Just like that, he was ready to put me to work at club Uno.

I said, "I had no intentions of working tonight. But probably tomorrow." I didn't want to admit it in front of them, but I wanted to take care of business with my body first. So I drove back home, shaved my pussy hairs real good, took a shower, got dressed and drove right back to Uno to work.

When I walked back in that early afternoon, Pete was surprised to see me. He said, "Shit, I thought you said you was coming back tomorrow."

"I changed my mind," I told him. The truth was, I wanted to get that money immediately. So after I drove back home shaved my pussy hairs like he told me too, what the hell else was I waiting for?

Pete escorted me into the back dressing room, while I imagined what he *really* liked in a woman. He had a serious sex appeal and power over pretty girls that seemed natural. He seemed like a boss who didn't take no shit.

So I had to make some rules for myself to keep my plans. Rule number one; I told myself, *Don't ever fuck with the manager, the DJ or the security.* Because any of those guys can try to get you if you're not up on your game. Guys are guys, you know. I also told myself, *Never interfere with any bitch making her money.* I knew I didn't want anyone interfering with my money, so I didn't want to interfere with theirs. And those were my main two rules. Another rule was not to get involved with the guys who liked to hang out in clubs. But I'll talk more about that later.

When Pete finished walking me to the back, I went into the dressing room and looked around at the other dancers, who were there getting dressed. There were some pretty bitches in there working dayshift, but I could tell that a lot of them were older though. They were still trying to hold onto to that big club money. I called the older bitches "madams"—women who had been doing their thing for so long that they knew all of the rules already. Shit, some of them older hoes thought they could make their *own* rules.

I was the new hot bitch in the room and the youngest, so usual, some of them started eyeballing me and whatnot, but I wasn't there to make friends with anyone. The game hadn't changed for me. I was still there to get that money. That's why I had come back so soon. But this one bitch who continued to stare at me had the word BEEF tattooed across her ass in big bold letters.

I was thinking, *Oh God, I hope this isn't another Princess.* This bitch reminded me of the jealous-ass hoe at the first strip club that Vicky and I danced at in South Miami. But at least this old bitch didn't say anything to me. She only whispered to one of the girls as we all changed into our costumes.

I knew she was talking about me, but ask me if I gave a fuck. The money that I planned to collect didn't have anything to do with those bitches. But that Monday was slow so I only made three-hundred dollars. I had worked a good amount of hours from one o'clock until eight that evening for that little bit of money. I wasn't used to that. Three-hundred dollars wasn't enough for me.

I packed up my bags and headed out the door for my car and was *pissed*. I mumbled to myself, "Is this the place where Louis said I could make the most money?" It sure didn't seem like that shit to me.

Before I climbed into my car and drive off, Pete approached me from behind, smelling like a million bucks. He knew that he was around pretty, half-naked women all day, so he had his pimp game down to a *science*, I was sure.

He said, "Today was kind of slow, but it's usually much better than this. I want you to come back tomorrow."

Pete was trying to entice me with his smile of perfect bleached white teeth, *gleaming* at me. But I really had to think about it. I was already spoiled by the money I had made on the regular and The A, so I was tempted not even to go back to Uno.

When I drove home that night, I felt like I had a big decision to make. The guys I knew at The A in North Miami always made sure I got paid at *least* seven or eight-hundred dollars every night. But at club Uno, I didn't make *half* of that. Nevertheless, I gave The Uno another shot and showed up that next day, ready to work even harder. I realized Uno was a top of the line strip club and that I wasn't the only bad young chick working there. So I had to deal with and learn to complete. Things don't always come so easily in life. So I bit the bullet and went back in there.

On my second day there, I pulled in my normal eight-hundred dollars. That was what I was more used to. That wasn't as bad anymore for the day shift. But I learned fast that I would have to make my presence *known* at Uno and build up my own clientele. I had to make new customers *ask* for me every time they walked up in the club. I didn't have to do all that at The A because the guys already knew me there, but at Uno, I had to start all over again and build up my rep. So that's what I began to do. I wanted to make Dior one of the hottest bitches—if not *thee* hottest bitch—at Uno.

But while I worked to break in during the dayshift, I kept hearing the night shift girls coming in bragging, "Bitch, you missed it last night. It was green carpet money everywhere."

That was the dancer's way of saying it was a lot of green money on the floor from customers making it rain. I already knew that the night shift was where the real money was. No big real big-money niggas went to the strip club during the daytime. The dayshift was for the low-money niggas. So I wanted in on the night time action and *fast*.

The first thing I did was consider my body compared to the other girls that I had to work and compete against. Overall, I had a nice body, but my breasts were small, like the size of Jada Pinkett Smith's. I had a size 32-A and that wasn't working enough. No offense to Jada, but I needed something more than that to compete against the other girls on the night shift. You had to show and prove in the strip club every night. So it made me start looking at my body differently.

A lot of guys in the club seemed to like my small titties. They weren't bothered much by what I was working. It was what it was. But *I* wasn't feeling my small titties. I wanted more to work with. I mean, you had over *fifty* other strippers working and competing against on different nights and shifts in the club, so I couldn't go out like that.

I heard a stripper in the club named Blaze had just gotten her boobs job to blow up her shit, and I was right up on her to get the information for the doctor. So I stepped to her inside the dressing room.

74

"Hey, Blaze, did you get you boobs done? Can you give me the number to the doctor?"

A lot of the girls were getting their titties or asses done to compete, but I didn't need an ass job. My ass was already fat, round and perfect.

Blaze said, "Oh yeah, girl," and gave me the hookup to the doctor. Blaze was an older madam who didn't waste time on the hating and jealousy shit. She was tall, slim and chocolate with titties that looked good on her body. She told me she had looked for a year and a half to find the right doctor to do it. And she and this other madam named Sun Kiss had gone to the same doctor.

Sun Kiss was the opposite of Blaze though. She was short, light skin and banging with big ass curves. Her club name fit her ass to a tee, like guys had been kissed by the sun when she danced for them. So when they both told me that this doctor was the one, I was all in on it.

The plastic surgeons name was Dr. Peter Summers, a cool and calm, white man who had an office in Miami Beach. And when I first went to his office for my consultation, he had a strong assessment and compliment of my body.

He said, "You are already tall and sexy, so I would advise you to get no more than a three-C." He said that would look the most natural for me and accentuate the rest of my body perfectly.

He showed me a sample of a 3-C implant inside of a bra so I could see how it would look. And let me tell you, I was so excited to enhance my shit that I put down a two-thousand dollar deposit that same day.

Money was not an issue for me. I was still making it just not as *fast* or as *large* as I wanted it. These Miami guys *always* had money for ass and tits. They were taking money away from own families to pay us, but that was their problem and my good fortune. The money had to go somewhere. So in just two weeks, I had new 34-C boobs to match my ass and to work with every night.

Call it superficial if you want, but with these new titties, I felt like I could conquer the *world!* It's like a guy with new money in his pocket. And I wanted to make a name for myself at The Uno without having to fuck Big Pete to make it happen. I was being invited to dance for the night shift all of the time. But I wanted to make sure that I was ready first, because the night shift was a totally different kind of crowd.

It was pretty laid back during the day shift, but the night shift was rowdy with way more girls, noise, people and shit popping off. So I just wanted to make sure that I was ready to step up my game like that before I went up there to make my money. I didn't want to go to night shift and then realize that I was overwhelmed by the shit. I wanted to take that shit by storm when I did it.

Despite Pete's first rule of not fucking the manager or the night time DJ plenty of strippers were fucking him to get ahead at Uno anyway. I guess that's how he warned them not to talk about it. But of course, I heard about it all anyway.

My girl name Diamond joked one time, "They must think he has some good *dick* if all these hoes want to keep fucking him in here."

Diamond had fucked him too, right in his back office. She told me so herself. She was older than me with a dope-ass body. I thought she was the *shit*. She could tell me anything she wanted to. I had to respect her game. And she didn't give a fuck about what anyone had to say about her either. She was hard-ass bitch. I guess that's why the called her Diamond.

I asked her, "He did that right up in the *office?*"

I was still a new dancer and one who hadn't been with a lot of different guys in my life. I was more about that *money* than sleeping around these wild-ass niggas.

Diamond told me that one of the older madams

named Moist had set it up for her to fuck Pete in his office like a freak, and that he gave her five-hundred dollars for it. She said it was only a one-time affair and that I shouldn't tell anyone that she told me. Just from how she was acting, I could tell that she was still fucking him on the sly. She just didn't want it to get back to the older madams in the club, who were still strung out over Pete.

The older madams were more trustworthy for his management, because they kept coming back and knew how to work it. But a lot of the young and inexperienced girls would excite the club and then leave to do other shit. So you couldn't count on them as much. Some of the new girls were easier to get turned out by the superstar VIPs who walked into the club too, where the madams kept their shit strictly business. So Pete never let his madams go. They were more loyal to him.

For a lot of the girls, fucking Big Pete was strictly business for them too, but some of them really loved him. Nadia—a pretty bartender at the club—had been his bottom girl for *years*, but he also had this young girl named Faith that he was secretly fucking. Or I guess it wasn't secret *enough* because Faith and Nadia began fighting in the middle of the floor one night. And this girl was only eighteen or nineteen-years old. So he was breaking *all* the rules for her to begin with. It was purely disrespectful in my opinion.

I guess all the paperwork they had us to sign was only to look like they were on top of things. But I don't know if these younger girls were lying on their paperwork with fake IDs or not, but we all knew who wasn't legal in there. Anybody could tell.

You always knew which girls Pete was fucking or showed favoritism to, because he would have them lined up at the night shift—front and center—to get money whenever his VIP guests came to the club; the professional basketball and football players, rappers, big time comedians, movie stars and all of that.

I could have fucked Big Pete to move up the ladder myself, but I honestly didn't feel the need to. I was building my name already and making my own money the hard way. *Good* money too. But I still wanted in on that night shift. That's what I got the boob job for and Pete notice it too. I still didn't pay him any mind though. My father told me to have a plan and that's what I was sticking to.

Pete never said it to me directly, but you usually know when a man wants to fuck you and I was sure that he *did.* Then he started getting bold about it by whispering in my ear.

One time he teased me, "You know I want you." But I continued to ignore it all.

Then he would walk up behind me and grind on my ass. Sometimes he would run his fingers across my hands and run hundreds of dollars across them. He knew what we all wanted and he was fine as hell to boot, but I just couldn't do it. I had my *own* rules to abide by and they included not fucking him, the DJ, the security or any of the VIP guests, who came through the club. I just *refused* to be turned out by the strip club lifestyle, like a lot of the other girls were. So I fought to keep my mind focused on the money and nothing else.

Big Pete was a tough businessman who knew what he was doing, but he also got away with breaking his own rules to get constant new pussy. He just loved to fuck new girls, I guess. So every time a new dime popped up in the club to work, she became another target. I didn't want to be a part of all that shit no matter how sexy Pete was. So I never allowed myself to fall into temptation.

After my first month or so of figuring things out, I felt that I was ready to move up to the night shirt. I guess he realized that he couldn't fuck everybody, and I could make him more money on the night shift as a pretty new face with big tits and ass. That's what a quality strip club is all about; hot, new bitches and the old pros to show you the ropes. That's how you keep the money rolling in from loyal customers.

By the time I started working night shift, I was feeling myself. I knew that I had *earned it* without fucking anyone and I was ready for it. So I stepped up that first night with an ass so fat I could barely fit it in my pants. I wore a pair of gold, thigh-high boots and my brand new titties up in the club as the DJ called my name.

"Welcome, to the stage—*Dee-orrr!*"

I looked out at the night shift crowd of big-money niggas as was nervous as hell again. It was a much different kind of crowd. The night shift was wild and just right for making more money.

My girl Diamond whispered in my ear to help me out, "Confidence, bitch. Move like you're the only bitch up in the room."

I *loved* my girl, Diamond. She really had my back in there. So I listened to what she had to tell me and it *worked*. The guys gave me their full attention and the bigger money started rolling in. On an average night, I made about the same money I was made at The A, $1,200 to $1,500 a night. But on the special nights at The Uno, You could $2,500 to $4,000 and no one was scared to come.

But everyone wasn't cool with me making the decision to step up my game in the strip clubs. Obviously, people started talking about it. And the more popular I got, the more people talked. That's when Queen—one of my oldest cousins—told my father that I was out stripping.

When I first told my cousin about it, I thought she would keep it to herself. We were just having some average girl talk when my cousin started talking about the strip clubs and so I told her I was dancing. It was just a private talk between me and her and she was older than me so I was confiding in her as a mature family member. I had no idea she try to tell anybody about it.

But after we had a petty argument over some borrowed luggage, she couldn't keep her big mouth shut. So she told my father about that I was stripping just to spite me, which was some immature, young girl shit. My cousin was like, six years older than me and she was still acting childish like that.

First of all, I let her borrow some luggage of mine after she asked me if she could use it. But then when I went to get it back, I guess she thought I had given it to her to keep, because she got mad when I wanted my shit back. You believe that craziness? Some people are that *pressed*, even your family members.

So she went ahead and told my father and then tried to be slick by warning me that she told him. I don't even know how she started talking to my father about it, but I didn't care. She should have known better than that shit.

Once Queen let the cat out of the bag, I was like, "So what if my dad knows? What is he gonna do, *beat me*? I'm a grown-ass woman now! I don't have to answer to anyone!"

I didn't have anything to lie to my father about. I wasn't afraid of him or anything. And all I could think about was my cousin Queen's disloyalty and how she had acted like a petty child. She had a lot of things going on about her own life that I would never tell and I just didn't want her to get the last word. That's the difference between me and a lot of other people that I know. I've always been loyal like that. So out of respect to my father, I decided to tell him the truth. It wasn't like he was never going to find out. I mean, I *was* stripping.

I told my dad like a soldier, "Yes, It's true. I am dancing."

Even though I had a lot of anger still left in my heart, I still felt like I could reason with my father and tell him anything. We had all been though a lot in our family

80

and he already knew all of that. He knew our mother had run away to Atlanta and left me there to deal with everything on my own. So my father listened to me over the phone for several minutes in silence before he finally spoke up.

He said, "Well, if you're gonna do that, then you need to have a *plan*. You can't just be stripping out there with no goal. You have to know what you want to do with the money; how long you're gonna do it and how and when you're gonna move on? You don't want to keep stripping for the rest of your life, right?"

I said, "Hell no. This is just a meantime thing."

My father said, "Okay, well, just be careful out there and stick to your plans to get out."

That talk with my father gave me more confidence to do what I needed to do. He wasn't tripping about it. He looked at it logically. So Queen's plan to start a riff between us had backfired on her and my father's advice actually helped me to focus more. I needed that focus too, because the complications of strip club game were just beginning.

The Strip Club Junkies

Strip club junkies are what we called the guys who liked to hang out all day and night at the strip clubs. Sometimes, these guys like to *forget* that we're professional dancers. That means whatever we do is strictly *business*. Some girls in the clubs forget that too, especially when big money is involved. Guys are constantly propositioning you to do more than dance. They try to get into your personal life, and I have to admit that I was tempted a few times. But I was always very picky about the guys that I got involved with personally. I've *always* been that way. And I couldn't see myself with the guys who liked to hang out at the strip clubs. I always thought they would do anything they could to get with anybody, and I was *right*.

One time I had a guy who gave me two-thousand dollars for dancing. I was in such a zone that night that I didn't even care, or at least I didn't *respond* like I cared. That's how you have to be. You can't let the junkies know that you're too excited or they'll try to use it against you. You have to act like you get big money all the time. So I just kept doing what I was doing. But I damn sure didn't lose sight of this guy. I wanted to make him my steady customer. All he had to do was keep coming back.

I could tell this guy wanted me though. I had his ass locked in. This guy wasn't good looking at all though. He was in his late twenties and a little on the chunky side with crooked-ass teeth. But as long as he was willing to spend money like that, he was giving me something to work with.

Like I hoped, he started coming back to see me at

the club often and have me dance for him. He came about two or three times a week. All he had to do was give me the eye and I knew to make my way over to him. And he kept breaking me off with thousands of dollars until we eventually traded phone numbers.

The sad part about it is that I couldn't even remember his name. It wasn't even that important to me. But I know one thing, with all of the money that he had given me, I knew that he wanted some pussy. I was mature enough to know that big money don't pop in your panties for *free.* You had to *earn* that shit whether you looked at it that way or not. Girls that didn't see it that way must have had some real generous fathers. But I didn't, so I knew what time it was with this nigga from day one. The only question was whether I would give in to him or not.

So I called him up a few times and we went to hang out or whatever, but he wasn't the type of guy that I would just give the pussy to. I had certain rules about club niggas that I didn't want to break. Basically, I just didn't *trust* them. Who is to say that he wasn't out there trying to fuck other girls at the club and at several different places? I didn't know him like that. I needed to find out who he was first.

I remember we sat in his car one time after both getting our cars washed. He had a silver Mercedes Benz CL. We didn't go anywhere; we just chilled inside his car to talk for a minute. But he tried to stick his hands in between my legs to feel on my inner thigh and jam his tongue down my throat.

He started begging, "Kiss me, baby. Kiss me," when I was ready to leave.

I pushed him away and removed his hand from my leg, while pulling out my phone. "Sorry, baby, I gotta meet someone," I told him.

I was trying my best to play it off and get to know him better.

But he got mad and said, "Damn, you're just gonna do me like *this*?" and he pointed down to his crotch. The man had a hard dick already, like I was supposed to do something with it inside of his car.

He was coming at me like I was a common *hoe*. I rolled my eyes and kept my cool. I said, "Don't worry, baby, I'll make it up to you," just to keep him happy. I caressed his chest and softly kissed his cheek before I climbed out of his car. I hope he didn't think I was doing shit else.

When I walked away from his car, I told myself, "Child, *please*." He must have thought I was some young and dumb, but I wasn't going out like that.

I went home, got my stuff together and headed back to the club night for work. I don't what was going on that night, but all of the dimes were up in the building *early*. I guess we all had bills to pay. I didn't sweat it though. Once I made a name for myself at The Uno, nobody was getting in the way of my money. So I headed to the lockers to get dressed while keeping away from the rest of the messy hoes in the room.

I wasn't trying to be nosy, but I overheard one of the other dancers named Kelly complaining to her man over the phone about how much money she needed to make that night.

"Baby, I can't make that much in one night," she was whining.

The word in the club was that she had a pimp, who had another girl name Star as his main bitch or whatever. So he basically treated Kelly any way that he wanted to.

I felt sorry for the girl, but I couldn't really understand it either. I mean, why would you let a nigga pimp you when you're already in s safe place making your own money? It wasn't like she was out in the street and needed clients and protection. But I guess once a nigga got his hooks up in you, a lot of girls don't know how to break away from those kind of guys. That's why I made sure not to get too involved with guys like that. They knew what kind of money we were making up in there and a young, dumb bitch could become a guy's easy paycheck.

I shook off this girl's conversation and went on about my business in the club. I walked out on the floor and ordered my favorite drink before I got started—Patron and lime juice. I could really fuck up some Patron and lime juice and it all went down smooth, like I liked it. Then I got into my groove to make my money.

Like I said, the dancers were all there early that night but it took a minute for the customers to all show up. Once they did, I peak through the cracks and saw my guy Rodney who I was with earlier. I just knew he was about to break me off again. I was already counting my check. But he had a change of plans for my ass.

Before I could make my way over to him, he started dancing with big-nose Alicia.

I looked and told myself, "Fuck Alicia." I didn't sweat her ass at all. Alicia was no competition for me. So I walked straight over to my usually customer and said, "What's up?"

He knew what time it was. I was coming to get my usual paper.

But he was like, "Nothing, I'm good," and pointed at Alicia, as if she meant something to him.

I turned up my nose and said, "Really? It's like that?"

He pulled Alicia closer to him to make his point clear to me. "Bitch, I'm good, right here."

I was just about to say something else to his ass when he continued.

He said, "You saw me earlier today, right? And after all that money I spent on you, you gon' act like you still don't *know me*. So I don't know you know either, *bitch*," he repeated.

You know what? I smiled and shook that shit off. I had been called way worse than a bitch before, so I didn't pay that shit no mind. There were other niggas up in the club, so I figured that was *his* loss, and with leaky-ass, big-nose Alicia too. That girl couldn't keep her excitement in check. She needed a damn baby wipe in her boots. That's how wet she got for these junkie niggas. She had a man at that, but still got all wet for that big money.

So I brushed his ass off my shoulders and got to stepping. That's how junkies try to play you though, so you can never catch feelings for them niggas. They'll try to you dirty every time. That's why I didn't respect a lot of those guys. But it was all good. I let his ass try his luck with Alicia. And if she wanted to give him the pussy like that, then that was her business.

But to tell you the truth ... I didn't really have any beef with Alicia. That's just how easy it was for the junkies to have you bickering with another girl over your money. It's sad, but it was true and I wasn't above falling for the bullshit myself. I mean, I was only human so I responded foul when I felt hurt or disrespected like anyone else.

I had another guy named Flex who I learned to trust the most. Dark-skinned with a balled head like Jordan, Flex was down for me without sweating me about giving up the pussy. He understood that dancing was my *job* and respected me for who I was as a young woman. And everyone knew that he was married.

I had a lot of love for Flex. He was always in the club wearing dark sunshades, like he was the coolest guy in there. The other dancers liked to flock to him for his undivided attention, but he never lost sight of me. We had our cool little vibe together and I think he respected me more because he knew I had a plan with my shit. I was basically taking care of my whole family with that money.

On night Flex was in the club, chopping it up with me as usual, when these two other dancers, Brown Eyes and Diva invaded our space. I remember they weren't even dancing that night, but I guess Brown Eyes was fucking Flex and felt some kind of way about me talking to him and dancing for him. I had problems with both of them anyway.

Brown Eyes and Diva were the kind of women who tried to fuck with your money by walking up and dancing all around your customers and shit. And now they were trying to stop me from getting my money all together. So we were always going to have problems.

She started talking loud and boisterous, telling Flex not to dance with me. They were both older strippers who were past their primes. Hoes bicker with envy and jealousy even more when they get old and desperate. They know their time is up. And even with this woman's beautiful hazel eyes, she knew that she didn't stand a chance against me. I was the young hot chick that she *wished* she was.

Well, I wasn't into fighting and arguing and shit over a man who wasn't mine, so I was ready to move it along and avoid the drama. But then Flex grabbed my hand and told me to stay. So I felt more confident about and started smiling like I had just hit the fucking lottery. And it wasn't so much about the money; it was all Flex proving to these old hoes that they weren't as important to him as they *thought* they were.

The next thing I knew, Brown Eyes started ordering bottles of champagne for Flex's table with her own money, as if she was trying to send him a message that she *owned* him or something.

This crazy-ass bitch, I thought to myself. She was only wasting her damn money. Flex could have bought *cases* of champagne if he wanted to. Her antics weren't making an impact on that man. Then she started paying for other dancers, trying her best to keep me away from him.

Do you believe that shit? This bitch had lost her mind over this man. I mean, Flex was cool and all of that, but why blow your hard-earned money on a married man who's not even sweating you like that? That only reminded me to keep my head in there.

Well, the control game was on. Flex put a thousand dollars in my hand and told me to order more champagne. Basically, he was showing Brown Eyes and Diva that their little money wasn't worth shit. After awhile, I went with the flow and found it all funny. Brown Eyes and Diva were the kind of older women who thought they knew something because they had been around way longer than me. But as they continued to get salty, Flex kept spending money to show both them hoes that he couldn't be bought like that.

One-thousand dollars turned into two thousand and two thousand went up to *three*. And the DJ started calling out the name of Flex's crew, Big Bank, all as Brown Eyes and Diva learned their lesson. They had a nerve to try and control the show that night as if they had *boss* money and didn't. But once they realized that Flex was going all in like a real boss, them hoes couldn't take it anymore and left finally left the club. But that's the kind of jealous control shot that went on with a lot of strip club junkies and some of the silly-ass dancers in there. It was all a game to them, so you couldn't take none of that shit seriously or you would suffer the consequences.

Like the girl Kelly, she was just too damn young. She was another girl who had faked her age with a fake ID or whatever because I know she wasn't twenty-one. I even heard that she still might have been in high school. She didn't have her own car, place or anything. That's why she always needed money something, depending so much on this pimp. He would drop her off and pick her back up, and then I found out she was living in a house with him and a couple of other women that he had. And this guy was still young too. He was only in his early twenties like me.

Well, Kelly was always whining about needed more money. So she fell right into Moist's hands and Moist started setting Kelly up with customers on the side. Moist was another madam bitch in the club, who used to be a dancer, but she was now setting dancers up with these junkies as if she was own pimp. She was the same woman who had set my girl Diamond and other dancers up with Big Pete. We all called her Moist and she worked behind the bar with Nadia.

Moist was an extra large bitch, who used to dance but she had gotten way too overweight for it. She still cute in the face, but she might have broken a nigga's legs if danced for him now. Instead, she fell back behind the bar, like a lot of other washed-up dancers. Only problem was, Moist had got involved in everyone else's business as if she ran the damn strip club. Sometimes, she acted like she was fucking Pete too, but she wasn't. I guess that's why she and Nadia were able to get along without any jealous bullshit. But Nadia only worked there two or three days out the week anyway. Moist was at The Uno damn near every day.

The word in the club was that Pete had helped Moist to break a cocaine addiction and she still felt loyal to him. The girls told me that Moist was walking the damn streets with her shit hanging all out while high on cocaine. She probably did a few tricks out there while she was at it. So she respected Big Pete for saving her fat, addicted ass and remained loyal to him. She would do whatever he asked her to on the sly and all of it involved business with girls and junkies in the club. It was like their little side hustle that we all knew about.

Moist set my girl Diamond set up with a lot more than just Pete. Like I said, my girl Diamond just didn't give a fuck. She was all about her money. So she let Moist set her up with a lot of paid niggas who came through the club, and Moist would take a percentage out of her pay on the deal. I think it was somewhere around 15% to 20% from what I heard. She charged the same for all of the girls unless she figured she could take more from you. But I heard that some of these strip club junkies were paying Diamond up to good money to fuck her.

Diamond talked to me but not to a lot of the other girls in the club. She was more laid back and secretive. So I didn't bother her about it and I let her make her money. I didn't judge her either. I mean, my girl Diamond continued to look out for me and show me the ropes on what and what not to do so. So I still had a lot of respect for her. She was like my protection.

But shit, I can't sit here and lie like I never even *thought* about get other money outside the club. You think about a lot of things going on in the club. But that didn't mean that you had to do it all. So I stayed on the other side of the fence. And if I did decide to fuck a nigga from the club for money, it would have been on my *own* terms and not on someone else's. I've *always* worked on my own terms. I was confident in making my own money like that.

Usually, Moist would set up her deals while bitches danced onstage. And if a guy at the bar liked what he saw and he had money pay for it, Moist would introduce him to the dancer. She would only do that though if she knew you from the streets or knew of you and could feel you out. And Moist knew a lot of fucking people. She made it her *business* to know people. She even collected her own tips for that shit. Not only that, but if any money fell behind the bar while these niggas made it rain on you, Moist would pick it up and keep the money for herself. So she liked when bitches danced near the bar. It got her some extra change.

Moist never promised pussy to these guys outright, she would leave that part up to the dancer. But if she knew that you left with a guy that she introduced you to, she would dock your money for it and just *assume* shit, like you got something extra for doing something. It got to the point where girls who weren't even fucking these guys were having money taken away from them. So a lot of bitches started complaining to Pete about her, even the girls that he was fucking.

Pete never went against her though. He let Moist continue to do whatever she wanted. He did what my father used to do to protect a woman, "Moist said she didn't do that." But it wasn't like they had strip club lawyers or something where you could bring her up on charges to get our money back. And if Big Pete felt that you were trying to fuck up his game and his money, he could cut off the water on your ass and just tell you to go strip somewhere else.

So what was the point in complaining? You got your money and you shut the fuck up.

I couldn't really fault a bitch for how she chose to get her extra paper though. We all had crazy circumstances and family situations to deal with in life. That's why a lot of bitches were stripping instead of holding regular jobs anyway. The strip club money seemed a lot easier to get without higher education and all that. We all knew how hard it was to get a job that paid you any real money. A lot of women were pressed and stressed out to hold on to them, like I was with my low-ass-paying hotel job. So we all said, "Fuck that small-money shit!" and decided to strip instead if you had the face, body and nerves for it. But some women took it to the next level.

I remember this dancer we called O.G. Cocoa. She was forty-years-old and had a tight-ass body, like she was still in her early twenties. *Seriously*. This woman was *stacked* and had six damn kids. That's when I first learned that there were several kinds of strippers; those who danced for fun and would never leave the club, those who looked at it as a stepping stone to make a quick dollar and those who used the opportunities in the club to paid to by hoeing.

That was Cocoa.

This madam bitch had been dancing since she was sixteen-years-old and still had customers waiting in line at the bar for her, young *and* old guys. They would all wait for her to make her way back over to them after she satisfied her other customers. I met Cocoa at The A before I even made it to Uno. She would always tell me stories back in the dressing room of how many years she's been in the game and about all of her experiences, while stripping for so long. She even showed me her bag of Golden Magnum condoms.

Cocoa used to brag, "Bitch, this is how you make *real* money."

She was constantly talking about fucking junkies who came to the club for her. But I used to laugh at her, because I still made more money than her from my stage sets alone without niggas even *sniffing* my pussy. So I damn sure didn't need to fuck any of them.

Cocoa, on the other hand, was not really into dancing anymore. She was more interested in selling pussy and could have gotten herself *arrested* if it wasn't for the club manager at The A looking out for her.

Cocoa would scream out in the club, "Who's ready to get their dick sucked?" just to get a rise out of the junkies in the club. Then she would grab a bottle of Corona beer, shake it up until it bubbled and force it down her throat. And it worked every time. The junkies in the club would start salivating over her.

She kept saying, "Y'all hoes don't know how to make no *real* money." But she never influenced me with that crazy shit.

I remember before I left The A for The Uno, I saw OG Cocoa slip a condom on a customer's dick on the dark side of the room and slide it right into her pussy while she gave him a lap dance. Cocoa *owned* the dark side. And as soon as that song ended, she jumped up off this nigga and headed right back to the dressing room to clean herself up like it was *nothing*.

I couldn't *believe* that shit. To tell you the truth, I think that Cocoa actually *wanted* me to see her fuck a nigga in the club to prove that she was real about her shit and not just talking about it. You had a lot of people who liked the *talk* the game not really *walk* the game, you know. So I had to respect Cocoa for her realness. That didn't mean I had to do it and follow in her footsteps though. I had my own game plan to stick to.

That's how this stripper named Treasure got turned out at club Uno. She let herself get caught up in something that was much bigger than she could handle. That bitch Moist was constantly looking for desperate dancers that she could eat off of for her extra money. She would talk to a pretty girl in the club and find out if you had your nose open for pimps, alcohol, drugs, the high of the money or just fucking with the wrong niggas, and she would use that shit to hook you up with someone.

Now Treasure was a pretty-ass girl who knew all of the top-notch niggas. She got paid so much that she would leave the club with garbage bags full of money. That's what you did when you had thousands of one-dollar bills that rained down on you. Or you could keep your money on an account with the "house moms" who would count out the money for us and keep it all on account for you to cash out as fives, tens, twenties and hundreds or whatever. But most of that money she made were from her connects with Moist after locking Treasure in with the big time niggas who were about that street life. And those guys had plenty of money to burn through.

I can't even name any names, because I still have to live. But Treasure got involved with this other stripper in the club named Dino, who put her on to some top street niggas. From there, Dino ran Treasure through the game out on the streets with Moist getting hers on the back end.

Moist knew a whole lot of street people because of her years as an addict herself. And the shit got so big in a drug money bust the club that Treasure was pulled into a grand jury court case, where she was asked to drop names and snitch on people, but she refused to it.

Going out like a soldier who wouldn't talk, Treasure ended up getting five years in federal prison, stripping her back down to *nothing*. And the word was that Money and all of her street connections that Treasure went to jail to protect, didn't give her a damn *dime* for her loyalty and let her ass go broke in jail. So when she got out she had to start all over again after losing five years of her life.

So even though club Uno had a lot more money to play with, I decided to stay in my lane and keep dancing and playing sweet head games for my money instead of fucking niggas. The bigger money for pussy caused way too many problems. So I left those strip club junkies alone.

VIPs, Money & Drama

The VIPs are the guys and sometimes women who made the night special and were treated special when they walked into the club. The Uno didn't really have a separate VIP section though. That's what made it so special to be right up close and personal with some of these celebrities who walked up into the club. They could be anyone from football and basketball players, rappers and singers, actors and comedians or just guys and women who liked to spend big money in the club for a good show. I felt like The Uno was every athlete or celebrity's second home in Miami. That's how much they loved to hang out there. Big Pete and Moist would make sure we knew who they were when they came in too, because the strippers wouldn't really know sometimes. I didn't know who some of these VIPs were either until somebody would tell me.

I remember this one famous football player used to come and hang out at the Uno like two and three times a week. It seemed like he was there every other day. He was an older, retired legend, and he wouldn't really spend a lot of money when he came, he would just come and sit right by the stage, smoking his big cigar. They all *loved* when he was there and nobody would bother him. The guys all looked up to him from watching him play football when they were all growing up as kids. So whenever he came in the club, they treated him like family, like he was everybody's big uncle. And he had been coming to The Uno like that for *years*.

This football legend had moved down to Miami

from New York and had mad respect in the club with no beef, but everyone knew that he was a *freak*. He didn't try to hide it either. He had a wife at home and everything, but he would still show as the club and act out. He even slept with a few of the girls in there, but I wasn't trying to fuck with him like that. Whether he was a big time celebrity or not, I had to keep my mind right and stay out of the bullshit to get my money.

This one time when I was dancing onstage, I didn't know that he had snuck up behind me when I felt someone's tongue in the crack of my ass.

I jumped forward and yelled, "What the *fuck*!"

I turned around and was shocked to see that it was him. I was ready to tell his, "What the fuck is your problem?" But I already knew that everybody loved him in there.

Big Pete, Moist and the security wouldn't have said shit about it. They would have just told me to keep my ass dancing and ignore it. Some of the other bitches thoughts it was cute and would let him get away with that kind of shit, but I didn't like it. So I went to wash up again and stayed away from his for the rest of the night.

This same football player ended up getting into trouble with this underage girl in New York. A pimp set him up with her to eat her out at a hotel or whatever, but the girl dropped dime on him and it ended up all over the news and courts.

I was like, "Yup, y'all see that shit." It was only a matter of time before somebody checked his ass—in my opinion. Just because you're famous don't mean that you can do whatever you want and get away with it. Eventually, it's going to catch up to your ass.

Once that that happened to him in New York, he started lying low and didn't come to the club for a long time after that. But then he started coming back again but not as much as before. He didn't act all wild like he used to before either. I guess he was embarrassed at being caught up like that and had learned his lesson.

There were a lot of VIPs getting twisted up in the strip club lifestyle like that. Those guys were hardly immune to anything. The fast life and easy access to money and sex can turn anybody out. But since we were in Miami, where they had a lot of professional and college football players that Big Pete and Moist knew personally, they were always in and out of the club and getting involved with the different girls who worked there.

There was this other football player who liked to hang out at The Uno who was worse than anyone. He was a popular wide receiver and one of those kinds of guys who liked to be all up in control of his women. He was originally from Miami and was a lot more involved with the strip club girls on a personal level, to the point of trying to intimidate them. I guess he thought that since we were strippers and that a lot of girls had personal issues or whatever, he could treat them however the hell he wanted to.

Now this younger football player still had some money, so he would toss it up lavish and make it rain for you, but he definitely expected something out of it. He would mainly dance with the girl that everyone knew he was fucking. He was the type of guy who would go after girls who he knew were easy pickings too. So if you had any money problems or were vulnerable to being infatuated with his football money and lifestyle, or were easily influenced or whatever, then you definitely had to watch out for his ass. Then he would have all kinds of beef with these girls if they didn't do what he asked or wanted them to do.

He was spending good money in the club and wanted to act like he *owned* these girls, like he was somebody's fucking *daddy*. That's how a lot of the celebrity types get when they have money and power. They can get way out of hand. He even tried to come after me at one point, but I was never attracted to him like that.

I was dancing onstage one time with this girl named Moet when he screamed, "Dior think her shit is too good! You act like your pussy is special!" He tried to make like it was a joke, but I knew he that he was serious. He was trying to see if I would break down for him.

"Actually, it is," I told him, laughing back.

I could tell that Moet was probably fucking with him too. That's why he didn't say anything to her. Guys like him would only sweat you *before* they fuck you. But after that, he would act like an asshole.

So I just ignored him like I always did with the guys in the club who tried to run game on me, VIP or not. And he knew that he couldn't really fuck with me like that so he never tried to bother me much. That's not to say that I didn't think about this football player. I just knew that he was already involved with too many girls in there, and that was a turnoff to me, you know. I mean, I had to *work* with a lot of these girls, so what I look like in the dressing room talking about the same nigga that everybody else was fucking? I didn't even trust where some of those girls in there had been. So, I didn't want this guy all up in me after being with any of them.

But just like with the older football legend, the addiction to the strip club lifestyle will eventually get your ass busted. So this younger guy ended up getting one of these girls pregnant and she took his ass right to court for child support payments. And again, since he was a popular football player and all of that, his court case and the money that he owed this girl was up all in the news.

I don't know why these celebrities always think they can get away with so much dirt, but that's how they were in there. Even though they were not out in the street life and didn't make their money that way, they still tried to act like street niggas. But they had a lot more to lose because more people knew who they were, so their popularity and good names should have been more important to them. But some of these guys didn't seem to care.

I felt the same way about the rappers. A lot of those guys really couldn't afford to be all out there in the street, getting caught up with dumb shit, like they rapped about. But it was as if they wanted to *prove* that were really hard like that and would be getting all fucked up in the lifestyle trying to prove it. But I can't even lie, some of these celebrities really were wild like that. Just because they had money and fame didn't mean they knew how to act or had good upbringing or whatever. Some of these guys had hard lives too.

Another VIP was a guy who I called Dread. He was a dark brown and stocky guy about thirty-five years old with medium height who I met when I first started working at The Uno. He wasn't really a celebrity like the other VIPs, but I treated him like one because he spent a lot of good money on me in the club and became one of my most loyal customers.

Dread was a regular businessman who owned an ice cream shop and he would come in and drop two or three "bandz," or thousands of dollars on me whenever he came into my territory. I would always see the jealousy and envious bitches eyeballing in my direction whenever he came to see me. But I really liked Dread because he knew what my boundaries were and how to act. He didn't let his money or his status go to his head or get carried away with anything.

Then this one girl named Passion, who I went to middle school with, tried to fuck up the money that Dread would spend on me. I mean, this bitch like really crossed the line. She wasn't even my age, she was a year or two younger than me, like my sister Charmaine's age. You would think that she would be cool with me since she knew me and my family or whatever. But this chick tried real hard to fuck up my money. That's one of my main rules—*never fuck with a bitch's money.*

Dread called me over to dance with him one night and she got all in the way like a Jill Scott song. I was already mad at her that night because I overheard her near the bar, trying to tell Dread not to dance with me. But Dread knew better than to listen to her, so he called me over to dance anyway. We had respect for each other like that and I could money from him anytime.

So I started to dance for him, and here comes Passion, sticking her little ass all up in the mix. Passion was like a Tomboy bitch who figured that she would do whatever she wanted to do and punk people. She was thin and dark-skinned, but she had that mixed girl look with all sharp features—a small nose, small lips, sharp eyes and she liked to wear weaves a lot. She was also bisexual, who was straight on some nights and a lesbian the next.

She would walk in the dressing room sometimes and say, "I'm only dating *girls* tonight." And on other days she would say, "I'm only fucking with the niggas tonight."

This girl was straight *crazy* and outspoken like that. But Dread didn't sweat it, so he got two-thousand dollars in ones and started tossing it up for both of us, and Passion tried to take all the money. I had no idea this girl would try to disrespect me like that. She was really bold. So I was ready to step to her about fucking with my money. Dread tried to stop me and told me not worry about it, but I couldn't let no shit like that slide, or Passion would try to fuck up more of my money in the club.

I confronted Passion about my money right out there in the open, because I was *pissed.*

I said, "Bitch, why you trying me like that?"

She grilled at me hard and said, "You tripping. That's my motherfucking money."

"Bitch, you know better than that. Don't pay with me," I told her.

She rolled her eyes and said, "Whatever."

Without another word, I snatched the bitch off the stage and threw her on the floor. Everyone looked at me in shock because I wasn't usually the one to make a scene like that. I usually handled my business and stayed to myself. But not that night! This bitch Passion was trying me as if I would let her get away with it. Everyone saw that she was grabbing up my damn money. So it shouldn't have been an issue for me to get in her ass about it.

Big Pete pulled us both backstage and gave it to us. "What the hell are y'all doing? You're supposed to be in here making money, not fighting and shit."

I said, "This bitch in here trying to take my money."

Passion said, "He was raining it down on both of us."

"Aw bitch, you know who he was in here to see," I snapped at her. "You and that damn bartender. I heard y'all plotting on my shit."

The bartender was some new girl and I didn't trust her ass either. But Big Pete didn't care.

He said, "I don't give a fuck *who* he was here for, I don't want y'all in here fighting. So I'm taking five–hundred dollars from both y'all and you can stay yours ass home for a couple of days."

Big Pete suspended us for a couple of days after that shit for my first suspension. Fighting and arguing was the main thing that management would tell your ass to stay home. It didn't look good for the club to have the customers seeing girls fighting and arguing over shit, you know. It made the club look ghetto and unorganized. But sometimes you couldn't help it. I can't just let some bitch walk up and take my money. That's what I was in the club all day and night to get.

Money was the main reason a lot of girls would fight—money and jealousy over niggas. But I wasn't fighting over any guys. That's why I tried to leave the guys alone in there.

After we both returned from our suspensions, Passion apologized to me and we moved on from it without any more beef or issues. I guess she just wanted to test somebody and found out I wasn't the one for that shit. When he would suspend you from the club, sometimes it would be for days, weeks or even *months*. Sometimes they would even charge you a fine to come back, like a thousand or fifteen-hundred dollars. They made you pay it all upfront too, before you could work there again. But girls would get that money up because they wanted to work. So if you had to work at another strip club to get it, then that's what you had to do. These girls knew that The Uno was still where the good money was.

One time Miss Piggy told a bitch not to come back at all because she caught her on camera dancing on a guy without her bottoms on. You could dance without your bottoms when you were on stage or not lap dancing, but once you start getting too close to a guy or tried to dance on him, The Uno didn't play that shit. Your club could be shut down for prostitution for that shit, especially at a club as popular as The Uno. So once they caught this same girl doing it a couple of times, they told her ass not to come back. She tried to argue about it, but they had her on camera. That's why they had cameras all around the club to protect themselves from the bullshit, whether it was the dancers or the customers trying to do too much.

Sometimes they even had to tell some of the *customers* not to come back when they broke the rules. Of course, that depended on who it was, because they still let certain VIPs get away with more shit when they were in there. Some of the madams—who had been working there for years—could get away with murder too. They would still protect certain girls and customers, because of the money they would make for the club or how much the customers would spend there.

At the end of the day, the money was what it was all about. But the management wouldn't let it too much out of hand. I mean, you still had to respect the business. Like the young bitch Faith, who was fucking Big Pete, that girl tried to get way out of hand too. I mean, she was hot and pretty, I'll give her that. High yellow and petite with a nice body, she had that Lauren London look. All of the guys wanted to fuck with her—young ones, old ones, hustlers, VIPs, *everybody*. And because she knew she was the shit, she would try and treat people badly.

This one time she took my friend's five-hundred dollars and told her she wasn't going to give it back to her. I mean, stupid shit like that.

I was like, "Are you gonna give my friend her money back?" I was ready to get suspended again for going ballistic on her ass, but she finally gave the money back.

Then she would have her mother coming up in the club, drinking and acting out, like a damn *fool* in there. Her mother would come to the club and yell, "That's my baby girl right there! That's my *baby*! *And* she's fucking the boss up in here!"

Her mother actually said that shit. That was so fucking embarrassing. I mean, who would have her mom coming up in the strip club, acting crazy like that and telling your business to people? But Big Pete would let this girl get away with all kinds of shit.

Faith got some of her medicine when she started talking bad about the DJ though. This one night she was calling him fat and ugly and was just *clowning* him for no reason. She went right up in his damn DJ with that shit too.

"You fat-ass motherfucker! Fuck you! And I wish you *would* touch me!"

So the DJ got tired off that shit and hauled off and knocked her ass right out on his steps.

I was like, "Damn!" and the club got real quiet. We were all in shock, thinking that the DJ was going to get fired or in some big beef with Pete, but he didn't. Big Pete turned the other way and let that young bitch take her medicine. That taught her ass a lesson that she couldn't get away with everything. Plus, the DJ kept the mood in the club going and he was a real crowd pleaser, so he was more important to the club than that dumb, young bitch thought he was. And you just don't disrespect people like that no matter how fine you think you are.

When you work around a bunch of five-star bad bitches like Faith, there's always going to be drama. That's just the daily shit that you have to deal with, so you learn to take it or leave it. When you have certain bitches making piles of money and other girls who don't, you'll have girls who are naturally jealous because they're not seeing money like that. And that kind of drama never stops.

I had to deal with all of those different issues on an everyday basis at the strip club. We had to constantly depend on these guys to spend their money for us to dance—however they got it—and we had to deal with however they would act toward us. That started to really stress me out, where I didn't want to be stripping and dancing as my only way of making money. So sometimes I didn't even want to go to the club.

Around that same time, my sister Naomi had her baby and I was still helping her to pay her rent and help out with everything. She had gotten pregnant by her Haitian boyfriend, but they weren't together anymore for him to help her out to raise their child or pay bills or anything. My sister had my beautiful little nephew and named him King. And since I had the money, we weren't trying to wait around to take his father to court for child support and all of that. We didn't have time for that shit. My sister and I both liked having our own money. So once Naomi was able to, she went back to work at the strip clubs while I would babysit for her and let her borrow my car. It was better than sitting home doing nothing, and the strip club still paid more than the other jobs.

My sister wanted to dance at The Uno too. She had known about the club and wanted to dance there before I even started working there. So we ended up working there together, but usually not at the same time. And folks didn't bother with my sister. She had that Queen Latifah size— but curvy—and she would knock a bitch out faster than I would. So it was no big deal to me that she worked there. We were both making money and I knew that my sister could handle herself in there with anyone.

But my other sister Charmaine wasn't into stripping or making her money that way. She was still living with my dad's family and working as a security guard. She didn't carry a gun or anything like that, she just wore a uniform at the Port of Miami with the boats and stuff and would have to report anything serious to the police or whatever. So Charmaine didn't even ask me for money anymore.

I don't blame her for not wanting to be a part of the stripper life. It's definitely not for everybody. It even drove me to start drinking. I started drinking like Vicky and so many other girls in the strip club just to pass the time, while coping with all of the bullshit. And what made it so easy was that these guys at the club would keep buying the drinks for you.

I would mainly drink Patron or Champagne and keep getting refills until I couldn't even taste it in my mouth anymore. You would just drink until your tongue went numb and then the time would fly by faster while you recuperated from it. I mean, sometimes you would be in the club all day and night with a bunch of regular junkies in there instead of the VIPs with the bigger money, and you would have to hang around until you made what you needed to make. The drinking helped you to do that.

But I learned my lesson early about drinking. One

time I drunk so much that I fell out in the club while dancing with this guy. They had to carry my ass in the back dressing room and let me sleep it off.

This other time I left the club drunk and had to pull over on the side of the highway. I didn't even know where the hell I was driving to. I ended up way out on the west side of Miami on Interstate 595. All I remember is being parked on the side of the road with the smell of alcohol everywhere. I was so damn tired and out of it that night that I had fallen asleep at the wheel with my seat belt still buckled.

I woke up when a Florida police car pulled up behind me with the siren on and lights flashing. The police officer walked up to my car at tapped on the window before I even realized what was going on.

I was like, "Oh, shit!" and it started me.

That's when I noticed all of the spit-up on my clothes. It was all down my chin, my neck and everything. My ass had thrown up on myself while sitting inside the car.

When I rolled my window down, the first thing this officer asked me was, "Excuse me miss, have you been drinking?" He was a tall, Asian-looking guy, built athletically and handsome.

With spit-up and shit all over me, I started trying to lie my way out of it. I said, "No officer, I was just exhausted while on my way home from work."

I was ready to say whatever the hell I needed to stop from being arrested for a DUI. But he told me to step out of the car. My heart started beating fast as ever as I climbed out, knowing that he would ask me to walk a straight line or take a breathalyzer test. But it was already obvious that I had been drinking. I was barefoot with tight-ass jeans on and vomit all over my clothing. I was a hot fucking mess in the middle of the night.

This officer made me to walk the line twice and told

me that I didn't pass. So I started pleading with him, "I'm so sorry, officer. I was just really tired after working late tonight, and I guess I had too much to drink or whatever. But that's why I pulled over. I'm all right now, though."

Then he asked me where I worked, but I didn't want to answer that. Cops don't always treat you right when they know that you're a stripper. Some cops even try to get over on you. Different dancers had told me plenty of slick shit about cops.

So I lied and told him that my father was a state official and that the car was in his name—
which was partly true. My car's registration and insurance was in my father's name. With my father being in his late forties, his insurance rates were much lower than the high rates they charged you in your early twenties. So my father let me put it all in is name.

But this officer wasn't going for any of it. I even tried to ask him if I could have his phone number to call him up or whatever. Since he was nicely built and handsome, I was even thinking about giving him some pussy if I had to. Shit, I had to try *something!*

But he was like, "Why would I give you my number?" He started acting all nervous about it as if I was trying to set him up or frame him. He wouldn't let me get too close to him either, but I guess not with spit-up and shit all over me. But I wasn't thinking about setting him up, I was only trying to get out of that situation without being arrested.

After all my begging and lying, the cop told me, "Get in your car and drive your ass home." I guess he didn't want to deal with my drama. But he didn't have to tell me twice to go home. I got in my car and got out of there. I couldn't wait to get home, get out of my clothes and get showered. Then I had to clean my damn car up too.

But that near arrest was a big wake-up call for me. I

had to keep the drinking in check before it got out of hand like it did for other girls.

This was all in my first two of years working at The Uno. I made good money and all that, but I spent it fast too. I was real irresponsible with my money, and that's ninety percent of the dancers. A lot of us had no guidance when it came to money. You would make it fast and blow it fast because it was too easy to get. It wasn't like my hotel job where I had to wait two weeks to see that shit. The strip club provided us with instant money, so you would instantly spend that shit, knowing that you could more of it right back.

I had nights where I would do a double shift in the strip club because I would come home and see a damn eviction notice stamped on my damn door. And it was not because I didn't make the money, I just didn't budget my money for what I needed to spend it on and *when*. I would just make money and pay for whatever I needed to right then and there, which became a bad-ass habit. You had to prepare yourself to stay on top of your shit. So it got to the point where I was always paying for stuff *late* that I would put off until the last minute. But I would always blow money on the material things that I wanted immediately—clothes, shoes, boots, designer accessories and plenty of hair. Hair was a *big* expense. I would change my hair up three and four time a month just to keep up that big life image.

I also tried to help too many people out with a kind heart, because I had money to give. Some people even thought that I had it all together and all figured out, but that was not the case. I was barely holding it together, just like they were. But the difference was that I kept going. I would never stop getting that money or pushing myself forward. That was just something I had in me from *God*. I would never give up on what I help I needed to do. But just imagine having to deal with all of the stress of a strip club as your everyday job. So I started to *hate it*. That's when I would think about quitting every day.

A lot of dancers thought about quitting but they could never do it or would never even have a *plan* of what else they would do if they *did* quit. It's hard to quit something like stripping when you know you can make thousands of dollars a night from doing it. There was no other jobs where you were going to make that kind of money without education and years of experience.

But every night was not about the glamour, the floss and lights in these strip clubs. What people failed to see is all of the crying and pain that went on in the dressing room at what we had to reduce ourselves to on a daily basis to get money.

Sometimes I would go home and just *scream* at the top of my lungs at all of the shit I had to go through with the *extreme* lifestyle that I was living. And a lot of the club niggas and haters would only make it even harder for you if you don't entertain the extra bullshit that they felt you should be open to. You have no idea how many guys tried to ask me to go home with them or to some hotel for some pussy. That's why dancers become so hardened when dealing with these people. We're *not* trying to fuck every man with some money who walks up into the strip club. Dancers are not fucking prostitutes! So when a lot of girls acted that way, they would fuck up the perception for most of us who *don't!*

I still have to admit that it's very hard for a girl to leave all of that fast money that you can make, while getting caught up with it. I mean, it really is an *addiction*, but I just *knew* that there was something else out there that was better for me. But when you don't have any direction, quitting can be nearly impossible. That's why so many madams who have been stripping for twenty years or more.

I had nights where I felt so lost and confused that I

started writing things down that I could do to still be my own boss and make god money without having to take my clothes off or allow strange guys to lust over me and touch my body.

That's when I first started thinking about my own business ideas, like promotions or even a female bodyguard service. I had this idea for some of the VIPs, where they could have a pretty girl with them who was armed and trained to use a gun, incognito. Sometimes people didn't always want those big, beefy guys around them like that. My idea would allow them to have protection that was sexier. So a female security business was one of the first ideas that I came up with. I guess I got the idea from thinking about my sister Charmaine being in security. I was even required to have a security license to work at the front desk of the hotel I worked at. But we still didn't have a license to carry or use a gun though.

Then I thought about my own party and event promotions business with marketing and stuff, because I was always around those people anyway. People were always promoting parties and shit at the strip clubs. They would know all about who was coming to town and who was doing what before everyone else even knew about it. A lot of times the celebrities who came to Miami for events would end up at the strip clubs anyway, from P. Diddy, Jamie Foxx, Young Jeezy, Gucci Man, Warren Sapp, Chad Ochocinco, Little Kim, Lisa Raye and more. At one time, Gucci Man and Young Jeezy would be up at The Uno, like every other week.

Since I was always around people who did the promotions to bring those kind of people in, I always thought about copying what they did and promoting events like that for myself. It just didn't happen right away. I still had some growing pains and shit to go through first.

A Break From Uno

When I reached my third year of working at The Uno in 2010, the club had a down period where it wasn't as hot as it used to be. I think the whole American economy was in trouble at that time. And it was during the summertime where a lot of the strip club crowd was weak. And with me having thoughts about quitting and starting my own business, I needed a break from The Uno and started working part time at the front desk of another hotel chain, while trying to figure things out.

While shopping at the grocery store I met this guy named Bernard, who I became casual friends with and started dating, who didn't know that I had been involved in dancing and stripping. He only knew that I worked at a hotel at first. It wasn't like I was broadcasting my dancing and shit. So he only knew me as Keisha and not Dior.

Well, Nard was a regular Miami guy who had friends from the Virgin Islands in St. Thomas, and he started talking about the strip clubs down there one day. So I finally revealed to him that I used to strip and still did it to pay bills when I needed to. I mean, I didn't stop dancing altogether, but I wasn't out there as much as I used to be. And I wasn't dedicated to The Uno anymore either.

Well, once I told Nard that I used to work as a stripper and still knew a lot of the girls, he guy told me that he had a friend who ran a strip club in the islands and that they would give me a hundred-fifty dollars to refer dancers to come and work down there to St. Thomas to work.

I was like, "All right, bet. I'll check that out." But I

just didn't want to refer other girls; I wanted to make my own money down there. I thought it would be something different.

So I recruited my girl Diamond and another dancer named Entice and went down there to the Virgin Islands in St. Thomas. The strip club was called Island Cove and the people down in the islands were way more peaceful and respectful than the hustlers that we were used to Miami. The regular working guys in St. Thomas loved American women too. So we all liked it down there immediately and knew that we could make some money there.

As soon as I got down there to the Virgin Islands, I noticed that this guy Nard lacked any ambition and was still at home with his mom in Miami. I felt like he should have been trying to do more with his opportunities, but he wasn't. I mean, how are you going to tell me about getting some easy money that you're not even trying to get? So we kind of fell out of contact with each other and I moved on from him.

This place Island Cove in St. Thomas was about the same size as the small clubs in Miami. They had a VIP room where you could grind on a guy, but no sex, and you could charge forty dollars per dance for a three-minute song. They had drug dealers and hustlers down there in the Virgin Islands too, but they weren't all fancy with it where they had to stand out and act ignorant like they did in Miami. You couldn't really make Uno money down there every night either, but what we liked about St. Thomas was that the guys were a lot more respectful and they were trying to really get to know us.

Their respect for us probably had a lot to do with us being American girls who demanded that respect from them though too. They still had some other girls at this Island Cove club who were from other countries and from the islands, who the managers and customers didn't treat as good. Some of these girls had traveled there from poor countries and Spanish girls who didn't have anyone to really protect them, so you would hear stories about the owner named Tony, holding onto their passports and threatening to report them to immigration and stuff like that. He was taking advantage of them and spoke Spanish and everything.

Tony was a big, heavy-set man who was not attractive at all. None of us American dancers were fucking with him like that. It was strictly business for us. He got some of the naïve, local and Spanish girls to flirt with him or whatever, but most his play came from girls who he knew were in some tough situations. He even tried to come onto me when I was still talking to Bernard.

Well, these girls in the Virgin Islands were more naturally beautiful and good-natured but they were not used to making the money that we were used to making in the clubs in Miami. American girls had that street savvy and hunger for money that demanded more paper and respect from guys there. They had a few girls there from New York and from DC, and the guys all knew who they were.

So I started traveling to the Virgin Islands St. Thomas and referring dancers there on the regular. Sometimes I would stay down there and make money from anywhere from a month to three months at a time. I would make sure I paid all of my bills and had taken care of my sister Naomi before I left. I would even send my sister two and three-hundred dollars from the islands through Western Union if she needed it while I was still down there.

But that's what I was willing to do to make my money. I still knew girls who wouldn't leave The Uno no matter what, even when they weren't making good money like that. And St. Thomas was a beautiful place with beautiful, hard-working people there. So I got a chance to see and experience something different while expanding my horizons.

I even had a chance to settle down in St. Thomas if I really wanted to. There was this Trinidadian guy that everyone called Trini, who liked to talk and spend money on me at the Cove. I remember when I first met him there, he was telling people in the club that he was looking for me.

"He's looking for me?" I asked the other girls inside the club. At the time, I didn't even know who he was.

But when I met him, Trini was so tall, chocolate brown and fine with long dreads. He was so rugged and fine that you would get weak in the knees just looking at him. But I was there working, and nothing go in between me and my money. So he stood there and checked me out as I headed to the front stage to perform.

After the first song, Trini took a seat right near the front and spent five-hundred dollars on me. I had seen more money than that from the guys in Miami, so I wasn't intense about it. But the other girls from the Virgin Islands had never seen a guy drop that much money on them at one time like that. So I had to tell them that it was really no big deal.

These other girls were from a lot of foreign countries with adverse poverty. But a lot of those girls wouldn't dance as long as girls did in the states. A lot of the girls in the Virgin Islands would end up getting married or moving on to regular jobs. They didn't make the kind of money from stripping for it to be much more than a meantime thing. So they didn't view the business side of it as strongly as American girls did.

When I changed into another outfit in the dressing room to go back out to dance went back, I told the other girls that I planned to make some more money from Trini, but he had disappeared. Oh well, it happens.

I still had to make my money and there were a

whole lot of other players in the crowd to dance for that night, especially for new meat. So I danced and kept making my money.

When the club was closing down at like five in the morning that night, I walked out to head back to the hotel where we stayed, and there was this black Jeep Wrangler waiting right out in the front, honking at me.

I was out of the country in unfamiliar surroundings, so I wasn't trying to find out who was up in this jeep. It could have been a maniac or anybody.

When the tall driver stepped up out of the car to let me see who it was, it was Trini. He wasn't flossing or trying to play big. His presence there was already known and the people on the island respected him.

He walked over and asked me to come home with him and that I wouldn't even to worry about anything. Just like at The Uno with Moist, this bartender in St. Thomas named Melissa knew everybody there. She told me that Trini was cool and wouldn't do anything crazy if I decided to go home with him that night. Melissa was from Trinidad too and had been over to his house for a couple of parties before.

I won't even lie, if we were back in America, I would have never even considered it, because I knew too much about how the guys were in America. But in the Virgin Islands, I had my guard down. And since Melisa had co-signed on it and knew Trini, I thought to myself, *Fuck it, just go ahead and do it.*

Even though I didn't know him, Trini seemed to have a very calm, island demeanor that was very attractive to me. They were a lot more relaxed in the islands than a lot of American men were. Trini just seemed trustworthy and gentle. I never felt that way with the strip club guys I met in Miami, even the ones that I liked. It was more about business when I liked them. But this guy in the island made me feel comfortable enough to make it personal. I just didn't have any fear that Trini would hurt me in anyway, whether physically or mentally.

So I went and climbed in his black Jeep Wrangler and we took off for his house late that night after the club. We didn't talk a lot on the way, I just remember him telling me he was involved in the music industry with singers there on the island. I didn't ask him a lot of other questions. I was tipsy that nigh too, so I can't even begin to tell you where we were driving to, but they have a lot of mountains and uneven land in the Virgin Islands, so we were going up and down a lot of steep-ass roads until we finally reached his house up on the hills.

It was late and dark and it was all about dick and pussy that night, so I didn't pay attention to a lot of the nuances. Again, it was like after five o'clock in the morning and all I remembered was the rocky-ass roads that we were driving on. We both knew what it was and it wasn't all romance, so I wasn't really paying attention to much. But when we arrived at his house, I stepped into a huge mansion, overlooking the entire island. It was beautiful and roomy inside. But we Trini didn't give me a tour or anything like that. We went straight to his bedroom and got to fucking.

I wasn't on some little girl shot anymore, so I took the dick with no regrets that night. I was all the way down in the Virgin Islands so I wasn't really worried about my business getting back to anyone. And it was a wham bam fucking and nothing to brag about. I couldn't even remember if we did it a couple of times or whatever because I was tired and fell asleep.

I woke up the next afternoon and looked around, wondering where the hell I was. A place can look different in the daylight when you don't really know your surroundings that well.

I look over and saw that a breakfast plate of potatoes, ham and plantains was sitting on a nearby table with orange juice, surrounded by hundred dollar bills. I don't know how long it had been sitting there, but I started to call and look around for Trini, who was nowhere to be found.

I climbed out of bed naked and started walking around the house while calling out his name, loudly. "TRIN-NI!... TRIN-NI!"

The house was so big and roomy, I could hear my echo. And it had a perfect view of the ocean down below. I mean, this house was straight up like some shit out of a movie.

I was thinking, *Damn! Look at this!*

I felt so comfortable in his house that morning and was walking around naked, looking for him. It was so quiet and peaceful inside that I felt that I could do that without it being a problem. Then I walked down a gigantic staircase, where every floor looked like its own suite.

I walked down another flight of stairs, while still calling out his name and checked into a bathroom for him. That's when I walked into a Jacuzzi filled up with packages of cocaine that were wrapped up neatly and stacked up high. I had never seen that much cocaine in my life. I had seen my oldest brother Pat Pat building it, but Trini had way more than my brother had. And this coke was just sitting there in the tub like nobody would bother with it.

At that point, I was ready to get the fuck out of Trini's house, thinking that it may have been raided by the island police or DEA or something. All I knew is that I didn't have time to get caught up in no bullshit over a guy that I didn't really even know.

Before I could close the bathroom door back, I heard his voice as he walked up behind him.

"What are you doing?" he asked. I could feel his erect penis on rubbing up against my booty before I could turn and face him. But since he had caught me looking in the bathroom at his tub of cocaine, my heart jumped, thinking that he would say something about it. I didn't know what he was about to do.

But instead of saying anything about the drugs in the bathroom, he grabbed me by my waist, dropped down to the floor in front of me and started giving me oral sex. I mean, he gave no warning or anything, he just did that shit. And it felt damned good too!

I started moaning and massaging his broad shoulders, "Yes, baby! Oh, God, yes! Yesss!"

Trini really fucked me up good with that. I must say, it was a very pleasant surprise.

Later on, I thought for sure that he would ask me something about walking into his bathroom and seeing the drugs in the bathtub, but he never said anything about it. I guess he wasn't even worried about it. He never even talked about it all, so I never brought it up either.

We started kicking it strong after that, and everywhere we went, people knew him in the islands. And he wanted to stop thinking about dancing. So every time we would meet up after that, he would greet me with a stack of twenty, hundred-dollar bills or more.

One time he showed me a stack of money and said in his thick island accent, "You see this right here; this is easily a hundred-thousand dollars. So you don't have to dance or work anymore." He said, "I got you. You have a kind heart. And I care about you."

From that day on, whenever I would spend the night with him, I would wake up and thousands of dollars would be waiting on the dresser for me. In fact, he never left with less than three thousand. That put me on *his* time so I stopped dancing when I was in the islands with him. He said that my dancing was no longer needed, and he meant it.

This new relationship went on like that for nearly six months. But then he would leave the island on business, sometimes for *weeks*, while never leaving me without what he called my "allowance."

The problem was, when I told him I had to leave St. Thomas to go back home, he didn't understand why. Well, first of all, St. Thomas was not my home. You know, I liked to get my hair done back at home, check in on my family, go shopping, see the familiar things places that I was used to—a lot of different things. I wanted to see my sisters, nephews, nieces—*everybody*.

The Virgin Islands were nice, but I wasn't trying to stay down there and get married or anything. Trini's house was big with a nice view, and he had good money that he was giving me and all of that, but I wasn't used to being set-up like that. I hadn't even known him long enough to make a decision that big. So as crazy and unbelievable as it was, like a dream man come true, I left for home.

Shit, I was a girl who had gotten used to doing things on my own, with my own money and my own space, so I just couldn't get into giving up my independence for a guy down in the Virgin Islands. I just wasn't going to do that. And I was still young in my early twenties too.

Before I left him there, he told me strongly, "Dior, if you leave me, then don't you ever come back here."

He was mad about it and having a grown-man's tantrum. I ignored it and left him down there anyway. But when I got back home to Miami, I missed him and wanted to go back, while thinking about what he told me and wondering if he really meant it.

Well, I return to the islands within a couple of weeks anyway, only to be devastated when I found out that he had already moved on with a another stripper out of the same club at worked at down there. He had started talking about me and everything, while going out with this loud-mouthed girl from Brooklyn, New York. I knew the girl from the clubs in Miami and it just tripped me out that he would do that.

119

That just went to show me how important it was for me to look out for myself. I mean, what if I did choose to stay in St. Thomas and he switched up on me over some petty, control shit? I would've had to start all over again anyway. So I did me and kept it moving.

Then again, I continued to wonder if I had made a big mistake by leaving him and only making it harder for myself again. But it was too late to change things. I had already chosen to go my own way. And I didn't feel as comfortable in the Virgin Islands after that. When you wear out your welcome, you have to know when to move it on, so that's what I did.

When I got back up in Miami, I wasn't trying to back to The Uno, but I did want to get back to my hustling and working at a hotel wasn't going to cut it—not after having a three-thousand dollar allowance in the islands. It would have taken me *two months* to make that much money back home on a regular job. So I wanted to step up my game and try something new.

I started working at this club called Dime Chicks in Miami Gardens near my father's people. But it was basically a whole in a wall place with a good name, so that idea didn't work out so good for me. I was just trying to mix it up and try to keep making money, but as soon as I got up in there, these petty bitches were hating on me and the money that I was there to make. That's how it is when a new bitch shows up at a club full of insecure dancers. I can't really blame them from a business side though. You never want a new chick moving in on your turf or whatever.

I was always on the quiet side, sticking to myself to get my money, but some girls took that to mean I was naïve or a pushover. But I was far from naive and weak. I just wasn't into that loud and petty arguing and shit. I didn't see the point in all that. You know, get your money and keep it moving. I never tried to hate on another bitch getting her money, because I knew that I would always get mine. You didn't even hear me talking about other dancers like that unless they had something they tried to pull on me.

Well, at Dime Chicks this one night, I ordered one of my new favorite drinks of Patron and sipped it down right before I was called on stage.

"Dior, Dior, you're up onstage next, baby," the DJ called out.

As I performed onstage, I could see that five guys were dancing three of the other girls, tossing it up and making it rain on them before one of the guys started tossing up money at me. And he tossed more money up on me than he did the other girls.

I could tell that one of the girls was upset about that shit, but that was the nature of the business. You couldn't tell guys how to spend their money in the club. They did what they wanted to do with it based on who and what they liked when they saw it. That could happen to anybody, so you really can't get mad at that shit.

But when I got ready to leave the club that night, I didn't realize how much tension I had caused just by getting my money. So when I went to pull my cell phone out of the charging in the wall, the same girl who had gotten upset at me for getting money while onstage, stepped on my damn fingers and said, "Wait 'til I get dressed," as if she expected me to be afraid of an ass-kicking or something.

This girl was my age or slightly younger than me and tall and petite. She wasn't no tough-looking street bitch or anything like that, so I was shocked that she even said that or did something like that to me. But I knew she probably had a lot of girls in that dressing room with her who was on her side.

My fingers were burning with heat, and I could tell that the entire dressing room was against me because I was the new girl again. So I turned and screamed at the whole dressing room, "Now bitches, I never fucked with no one."

It seemed like the younger dancers were the ones who were always trying to show there ass. And this girl named Toya was the only one who was not against me, because I knew her growing up in the old neighborhood.

But after I said that, this crazy-ass tall girl placed her finger right against my temple, still trying to punk me, and I fucking lost it. I went straight for this bitch face and got to swinging on her ass. Before I went off, they had two security guards in the dressing room with us, who were not even trying to break it up until I landed my first punch and knocked this bitch back. Only then did they jump in to stop it.

This big bitch outweighed me by a good forty pounds and all of her friends stated cheering her own as they followed me out of the dressing room with the security between us.

All the while, these bitches were still hollering, "Beat that bitch down, girl. Beat her ass." Those bitches were all from Broward County, so they stuck together like that.

I told Toya to come with me in case they tried to jump her for not being down with them, and it looked like a big-ass mob of strippers, fighting and arguing at close out time. That was exactly the kind of shit that The Uno wanted to avoid. That's why they would suspend your ass for it. But at Dime Chicks, I guess it was anything goes.

So as this big bitch followed behind me and Toya, I was on guard the whole time, just waiting for her to try and attack me again. And when she did, I grabbed her damn hair and pulled her down into my punches, smashing her in the fucking face.

I could tell that her friends were surprised that I didn't back down or allow her to kick my ass that night, so the security tried to jump in between us again and keep me from kicking *her* ass. I couldn't feel her punches or anything, but somehow one of her fingers landed in my mouth, and I tried to bite her motherfucking fingers off!

She started screaming, "Ahhh, shit! Get the fuck of me!" to release her fingers from my damn teeth.

That's when the security finally separated us to break it up again, while Toya made sure no one else tried to jump me.

The security told me, "Go ahead and leave, right now," as if I had started that shit. I wasn't planning on staying there after that shit anyway, *or* coming back there. I guess they thought it was all a fucking *game*, but I wasn't going for any of that shit. I had seen way more money than any of them bitches in there would ever see, and I would see even *more* too, so I was not getting my ass kick by any low-life bitches like *them*.

Toya left with me and we drove over to her house after calling my sister Naomi up to tell her about it.

Naomi was like, "I'm on my way there right now. Let's get these bitches."

But I told her crazy ass to just chill. I had already handled it myself and I wasn't going back there. *Ever!* That was just more of the bullshit in the strip club lifestyle. I sat there and joked while Toya about the fight that night, but in my mind, I still thought about how good I had back it in St. Thomas only for my ass to leave a damn *mansion* in the hills of the Virgin Islands—with thousands of dollars in allowance every day—just to return home for some petty-ass *bullshit* like that in Miami Gardens!

I was so fucking *pissed* at myself that night that I didn't even know what to do. So I sat there and drank some nasty-ass beers with Toya to try and forget about it.

With all that was going on with the Miami strip club scene, there really wasn't any money being made. Right when we had our first black President of the United States with Barack Obama, the money on the streets was drying up. I don't blame the President for it, but the economy was all fucked up and customers just weren't kicking out the money like they used to. Even the dope game seemed to be struggling. So I decided it was better for me to be in St. Thomas in the Virgin Islands—even if Trini was no longer my man. I made that decision after only two weeks back home. St. Thomas had spoiled me and I wanted to fly back there.

As soon as I returned to, I realized how beautiful the islands were. The first few times I went, I wasn't really paying enough attention because it was all about the money for me. But then I realized that it was a calmer way of life down there. I didn't feel the same pressures about life and getting money in St. Thomas like I did in Miami. Now, of course, I still wanted to get *paid* in the Virgin Islands, I just wasn't as pressed about it there.

So I returned to the two-story St. Thomas guest house in Bolongo, where dancers from all over the world stayed, while performing at the Island Cove. They were Chicago, New York, Miami, Trinidad, Columbia and more, and we all paid fifty-dollars a week to stay there. It was a huge guest house and no matter where we were from, we had one thing in common; we were all trying to *survive*. Some of the girls even shared bedrooms together with two twin beds for friendship, but not me. I came back to St. Thomas alone and I wanted to keep my own space. It also depended on your rank up in the club, and I was still one of the dime bitches to have my way there. So I liked to stay up on the second floor away from all of the foot traffic with a king or queen sized-bed. Call me a diva if you want, but it was what it was, and I was able to ask for and get what I wanted.

As soon as I flew back into the airport there—hot as fuck with no air conditioner—the people there already knew who were tourist and who lived there. So my fanciness stood out like a sore thumb.

Well, it didn't take too long for me to get settled again. I couldn't wait to get back to the Island Cove and bump back into my old man, Trini, planning to break some major bread with him. I felt that surely he would be happy and surprised to see me back. I knew damn well that Trinidadian nigga missed this Miami pussy. Or at least that's what I told myself. I had to make him want me again.

The Island Cove strip club there was nice and dark with a safe vibe and lots of neon lights, just like The Uno. I was able to appreciate it all more after coming back. Everything stood out more as I paid more attention to the smaller thongs. But I didn't have to do a lot of shaking my ass and spending up of energy in the islands. When they loved you down there, you could just walk around in the club and fucking *smile* and they would still love you. So they *loved me*, and I was able to appreciate them enough to love them back with my eyes opened wider.

I had major faces coming at me like the Queen Pen, but I was holding my ass out for Trini. I wasn't going home with anybody but him. So these new niggas were all hollering at me in vain. I didn't have to wait long for Trini either. He walked in the club that same week when I got back.

Once he spotted me, he walked right back up and asked, "Where you been?" in his thick island accent.

I smiled and played my seduction game perfectly. "Missing you," I replied. I wanted to act as if I had never left on bad terms with him. I wanted to act as if his new bitch never existed.

Trini went and got a bunch of ones and tossed it up for me in a heartbeat, as I stretched out on my back and spun my legs like a windmill, teasing the hell out of him with this Miami pussy again. The DJ was blasting Foxy Brown's *Tastes Like Candy* through the sound system, and I just *knew* that it was going to be on that night. I didn't

125

want to think about anyone but us.

I wanted Trini back with his money and the luxury that he could provide for me again. Like clockwork, he took me back to his house to spend the night, where I proceeded to fuck his brains out. But it wasn't like it used to be. I knew that our deeper connection wasn't really there anymore. It was just pussy and money now. I wanted to fuck him because I knew he would look out for me. That's just how he was.

So that morning, Trini drove me back to the guest house in his black Wrangler Jeep and dropped me off with fifteen-hundred dollars.

I returned to my bedroom upstairs at the guest house and lied down to rest up for another night of performing and getting money at the Island Cove. But I felt lonely without Trini with me. I felt like I was always by myself, but I had gotten used to it. All of my brothers were doing their own thing, my two sisters had kids and were doing them, my mother had moved away to live with her family in Atlanta and my father had his own wife and new family in Miami. So sometimes I felt lonely and disconnected.

I mean, I knew my mother and family loved me, but I had been going to get it on my own for so long that I really felt alone. It was all about the paper chase, twenty-four-seven for me. I think I was *afraid* of being loved, honestly. After my father allowed his wife to verbally and mentally abuse me in my adolescence, I just didn't trust a lot of people. Then I turned around and let a nigga abuse me physically and sexually as a young adult.

So there I was in St. Thomas, feeling special about my fresh opportunity to dance at the Island Cove again, where I had no hate and plenty but love. Many the islands guys wanted me there too. But no matter how much money they would flash in front of me, I remained very careful about who I gave my pussy to.

BEEP! BEEP! BEEP!

That was the small bus horn and signal for all of the girls to get ready to dance. The bus would stop right outside and wait for us out in front of the guest house. Then you would hear a bunch of different voices from all of the chatty women downstairs and outside. It was really interesting to hear all of the accents mixed in with Spanish, this island, that island and different states in the US. I really got a kick out of that.

The bus—the size of a large airport shuttled—held about thirty passengers and would take the dancers to and from the club each night. Imagine that, a whole bus full of exotic dancers from all over the American hemisphere going to the same club to dance for admiring men. But I felt like the Cove was my club.

My motto in St. Thomas was, "This is my house!" I really felt like I could do what I wanted to in St. Thomas.

There was another girl named Splash there too, a chocolate stallion sister from the Carolinas. I couldn't remember if it was North or South Carolina. This girl had a cute, dark brown face, thick body and all of that, but I could tell that she still felt threatened by me.

Splash was another one of those loud, ghetto chicks who liked to talk a lot of big shit, and like she knew everything. But I considered her harmless. She couldn't stop me or my money from flowing, so I paid her no mind.

Even the fat, nasty manager Tony knew who ruled the Cove, and it *wasn't* Splash. *I* was the one who got all of the guys hot there. Tony wanted to fuck me too, but it was not happening. I was not in the *least* bit attracted to this man, and I saw how slimy he treated the other girls who had fuck him, so I was not fool enough to go there.

I had the local customers so open in St. Thomas that I made this one guy come in his pants. I knew he did too, because I could feel his hard dick vibrate under me as he shook and grunted. And all I did was sit on his dick for a minute. I didn't even *dance* on him. That's when you *know* you got a nigga wide open. I didn't even have to *move* for this guy to come in his pants for me.

That same guy wanted me so badly that he begged for my number for the rest of that night before he left. So I finally gave it to him. I wonder how fast I could make him come again without doing anything and how much he would give me for that. And he wasted no time calling me either.

The next thing I knew, this nigga had pulled up to the guest house—where we all stayed—and he was waiting for me there. It seemed like all of the guys who had money and were willing to spend it knew where the guest house was and what they had to do to get some stripper pussy. But I was not the one for that shit. Like I said, I was very selective about my pussy and this nigga was straight-up out of control. I wasn't trying to fuck him just because he wanted me. A lot of guys wanted me.

So I climbed off the bus and ignored his ass on my way up to my room. He continued to call out my name, "Dior! Dior! Dior!" But my name may as well been *Thomasina* as far as that nigga was concerned. I was *not* trying to hear him. That made some of the other dances laugh at him and respect me even more.

I had been on the scene up in Miami, with some of the *roughest* niggas you could imagine, so dealing with a man in St. Thomas was *nothing* to me. Sometimes you had to put a guy in check no matter *who* he was. If you don't, they'll try to walk all over you. So I froze his ass out for a couple of days.

He was pretty persistent though, I'll give him that. He kept trying to get me until I finally let him make his offer. With the way that nigga wanted me, I knew I was about to get *paid*. I knew he was another island hustler and he drove a jeep too. That's what the big ballers drove in St.

Thomas. And they were never as flashy as Americans were.

Anyway, this guy begged me to come spend the night with him and said that he would make it worth my while. Then he gave me eight-hundred dollars right there on the spot! Well, shit, I started thinking about the other girls at the guest house calling me hoe if I did it, but some of those bitches were leaving the guest house with different guys every other night without any money in hand. So I said, "Fuck it!" and did it anyway.

I didn't feel good about my decision though, and I was not tipsy that night like the first time I went to spend the night with Trini. So I continued to feel apprehensive as I rode in the passenger side of his jeep. I just felt strange about it and was ready to keep my eyes open for anything unusual.

We pulled up to this white house, and he drove around and parked at the back of the house as we entered and went into his room. And the first thing he wanted me to do was give him head, like I was a porno chick. But this nigga was still sloppy from a long, hot day, so there was no way I was going to suck his dick straight out his jeep like that.

He said, "Okay, I'll go take a shower. Make yourself at home."

Unlike, Trini, this guy was short and thick, and as I walked around his house alone, I was not impressed.

By the time he was all showered up and clean, he walked out wearing a white bathrobe and feeling good about himself. Knowing that I was going to get paid, I sat him down in a chair and gave him a back massage before I squeezed and sucked on his nipples. Then I licked my fingers wet and started rubbing the head of his penis.

That move was my magic trick. I wanted to freak him out nice and slow and make sure that he wanted to see me more and give up the paper when I needed it.

Since he was all fresh and clean, I felt more comfortable about touching him. So I put some lotion on my hand and slapped it all on his dick and balls. Then I gripped him around his dick with a tight fist and started jacking him off with my slippery, lotion hand, up and down his shit.

You would think I had electrocuted this man with the way he started shaking in his chair. I mean, he went *crazy*, while calling out my name, "Dior! Oh, Dior!"

I had no intention of stopping until he bust a nut straight up into the air. Shit, it was his house, so he had to clean it all up himself. All I knew was that I wanted to turn his ass out without having to fuck him or suck him. And I wanted him to call me back as much as he could afford to pay me.

After he nutted all over the place, he wanted me to stay and cuddle with him and got upset when I refused to. I knew that I didn't have to cuddle with him. As long as I could turn his ass out, I would maintain the upper hand with him. I was only strung for more fast money and nothing else. So I told him I was ready to go back home and that he could invite me back over when he was ready to, which meant that I would leave my options open as long as he paid me, and I would continue to call all of the shots. He wanted to make it more serious than that, but I wasn't interested. I only wanted the money.

That's the kind of woman I had become. I felt like I needed more love from my father, brothers and family to be able to share love and receive love back. But once I had been out on my own in the strips clubs a few years—scheming every night to make a living from lustful men—I felt like there was no turning back. I would be hustler until that day I died. So I never took this man seriously and I honestly can't even remember his name.

Trini was still coming around the club and giving me money to sleep with every once in a while too, but like I said, it was never the same. I didn't stay with him like that anymore and it was all about the money. I had basically lost interest in him for anything more than that. He was no longer seeing the dancer from Brooklyn anymore either. I mean, it was what it was. Everything was about part time relationships in the strip club life, unless you left and hooked up with a man for real, which few girls ever did. Some of them would even get pregnant by a nigga and come right back to the clubs to keep making money.

I stayed down in St. Thomas at the guess house and made my money for about two more months before I returned home to Miami again for good. What can I say? I guess I got homesick. So I needed to find where I could go to go to make money in Miami again.

Things Going Down

I had to admit that I was attracted to dancing for more than just the money. I never felt so passionate or pretty as I did while onstage in front of a crowd. Up onstage, I was able to control everyone's attention, and I liked it. I felt sexy just walking around the club in my thongs. But after returning home from St. Thomas again, I couldn't work back at Dime Chicks. I didn't want to go back to Uno's at the time either. I wanted to try something new. Each new club presented a challenge for me. Could I be the shit again? I was curious to see if I still had it back at home. So I headed over to Primadonna's in Aventura to dance.

Primadonna's was a local money driven strip club in Miami that was neck and neck with The Uno for black dancer business. They didn't have a lot of celebrity business in there and they didn't care. Just like at The Uno, the local hustlers at Primadonna's would pack it out and make it rain on the regular. Aventura was also an upscale neighborhood where a lot of white people lived, but we still had a black-owned strip club there.

After just a few weeks of working at Primadonna's, the club manager and security guards were feeling me, not just as a stripper, but on the business level. They knew that I brought that extra hype to the club whenever I danced there. And I was always a good tipper. They would keep a parking spot in the lot for me when they knew I was coming and even carry my bags inside the club. That shit was *extra*, so I felt like a VIP bitch.

After all that I had learned in my three years of dancing at strip clubs—including traveling to the Virgin Islands—I knew to keep my body right, my hair done, my make-up on point and my attitude adjusted for making money. I knew how to wear the right scents too. Sometimes it took me a few hours to get my shit right for the club, including curling my hair. I was trying to turn my stripping and dancing into an art form, and it was working for me.

I was always big on presentation. You never know who you might see one night. Suddenly, I had a name around Miami and didn't have to wait on anyone's list to dance. New chicks had to wait and pay fifty and sixty dollars just to sign on the dance list. But I could pick and chose to dance anywhere I wanted.

The strip club game was still like the dope game— competitive and crazy. And if you wanted to be a five-star bitch, balling out like I was, then you had to do whatever you had to do. Fuck it, you had to pay the *cost* to be boss, like any other profession. So cute bitches thinking they could just jump up onstage and make thousands of dollars on the regular without keeping their game tight were fooling themselves. It may start off easy, for the first couple of months or whatever, but I had seen pretty bitches come and go a dime a dozen, who couldn't take a *year* in the game. So this shit ain't easy!

With my shiny, golden brown body that looked good in just about any color, I decided to make my strip club game *glamorous*, with all kinds of full body suits in red, orange, hot pink, floral and anything that set me apart for the average dancer. I wanted my shit to be a glam show every time, as if I was a Victoria's Secrets model. I made sure that every outfit hugged my banging-ass curves like they were tailor made, even if I had to alter them, which I did a lot. I wanted to make sure that my titties sat up like missiles and my ass popped out and bounced like hydraulics.

Getting myself ready to dance was always a process. I would take a shower, get my body airbrushed a golden bronze, my hair styled and curled and my make-up down to look just right. The process could take up to two hours sometimes, especially with the airbrushing part. I would do my legs, arms, toes, elbows and *everything* to cover up any scars or blemishes. So now you know one of the many beauty secrets of the strip club life—or at least for the five-star bitches. But it was worth it if you wanted to get that next level money in the clubs every night. A five-star chick had no room to slack off. You always had more girls on the waiting list who wanted to work, make that money and take your spot.

Stripping was just like the dope game. So if you wanted to be a VIP up in the club, you had to pay cost for it with your preparation. Then you could charge an extra fifty to sixty dollars a song to dance for a customer on *top* of your regular fee. Yes, the top dancers were making that kind of money, *easy*. And that's where I wanted to be.

There was another club I tried in Miami Gardens called the King of Donnas that tried to bank off of Primadonna's name. This was a much bigger club too, with fifty-thousand feet of space that the promoters and manager liked to brag about to get new customers. But Miami Gardens was still a crime-infested area at the time and you had to deal with a bunch of police cars out there every night to even get to the club. So a lot of folks were leery about going there. However, with all of the police around it made the club extra safe for some of the hottest new dancers in Miami, with celebrities showing up to boot, so the customers came anyway. And I didn't have to worry about fighting bitches there either.

They had these VIP rooms on the second floor that overlooked the club like skyboxes at a sports arena. I was curious to see what it would be like to dance there, so I tried them out to see what their paper was like. But we all called the place KODs to stop from getting the club mixed up with Primadonna's in Aventura.

I walked out on the stage one night at KODs, wearing all black with five-inch, thigh-high, black leather boots and a black latex body suit with my nipples cut out. I loved showing off my beautiful, round breasts. They were perfect. The bright neon green lights of the club were shining directly on me, spotlighting my twenty-inch, honey-blond highlighted hair. And every customer who walked toward the stage to tip me was caught in the lights. The spotlight color green was perfect for that. The presidential green backs was what I wanted.

I wanted *all* of my ass to show that night as I opened and closed my legs on stage, teasing customers with my ball-faced pussy. In my three years of stripping, I learned that pussy ruled everything. You just had to learn how to work it. But on that particular night, there were more women customers there than men.

Women customers tended to be more sensual than the guys were. So this one woman walked up and started caressing and rubbing my ass with hundred-dollar bills in her hands. I didn't mind it. By that time, I understood that some women liked women too. There's no way you can strip for three years around all of these five-star bitches without being around girls who like girls, so I had to deal with it maturely. Even celebrity women would come in and flirt with dancers.

This same woman that night had her man sitting right behind her as she asked me to dance offstage for her, while her man watched. So I danced for this woman, and she couldn't stop from touching and feeling on me, while sniffing my aroma. It was freaky shit going on that night, but her man seemed to be aroused by it. A lot of couples would come into strip clubs and let their imaginations run wild with a girl. Sometimes, they even offered you money for a threesome.

I remember thinking, *I hope these fucking freaks don't ask me to go home with them. We need to keep this shit right here in the club.*

I made a few hundred dollars with this freaky couple that night, but I noticed that KODs was pretty dry. They had all that extra space, but on certain nights, like Wednesdays and Thursdays, the crowd could be dry like any average strip club. A lot of the local customers were just not coming out or spending big on those nights. I guess they wanted to get their money right for the weekends instead. And on lot of Mondays, clubs would have these girl fight nights with boxing rings and everything that brought in a crowd of people. Monday nights also had that holdover money from the weekend. But I still had bills that were due that week, so I had no choice but to go out and go get it whether the crowd was slow that night or not.

That's when I first started thinking about promoting my own nights at the club. I knew that I could do better than the shit the club was doing, especially after taking girls with me down to St. Thomas. With the pretty bitches I knew from the islands, I figured I could pay to bring some of them up to Miami and show them how to keep it hot in America. In the meantime, I had to get whatever money I could get and continue to keep my name and game up.

But by 3 AM that night, I still only had a few hundred dollars to my name and I was *pissed* as fuck. I was ready to take my ass home and call it a night, but I *couldn't*. I had to make that damn money. That's when this tall, older man in his late thirties asked me to dance. He was dark, thick and fine as hell, favoring the actor Idris Elba from *The Wire*. But he didn't want the cheap dancing, all out in the open. He wanted a more exclusive, private dance in the small VIP rooms they had.

He was clean cut and smelled like Yves Saint Laurent cologne. But when I asked him if he wanted a lap dance, he answered firmly, "No," and pointed to the VIP rooms.

These VIP rooms overlooked the entire club, like luxury boxes in a sports arena. But I had never actually performed in one before. At the time, I was still pretty new to KODs. And to dance inside the VIP room would cost you three-hundred dollars for an hour before you even paid for a dance. So those rooms were only for the big ballers.

I thought an hour time limit alone with a man was a bit long myself. If I could make forty to fifty dollars for a three-minute song and dance out in the open, that would be more like *eight-hundred* dollars for an hour in a VIP room. So I felt that thirty minutes would be more like it for five-hundred dollars instead of eight.

Anyway, the club still wasn't jumping that night, so I agreed to lap dance with this older man inside of VIP room for the three-hundred dollars plus tips. An hour was the limit before you were charged another three hundred. So he gave me the three hundred and held my hand to lead me to the rooms. I usually didn't have to dance private in the VIP-rooms like that, but fuck it, it was his lucky night. I was ready for whatever to get it. I was distracted by my desperation to for money that night.

As he sat on a comfortable sofa in front of me, I wasted no time giving him a lap dance, while grinding my body hard into his dick to get him to pay me handsomely. I still needed to make some serious money that night, and I didn't have it yet, because the house money was not all money. So I pushed my titties all up in this man's face and let him smell my Burberry perfume.

This chocolate man sunk his head right in between my breasts and inhaled me deeply, as if I was a fresh cake at a bakery. He squeezed my body into him so tight that I could barely breathe. I felt his big dick good and hard underneath me too. You can tell when a man has big, long dick, and his was so big that it made my pussy wet. That was new for me. No customer was ever able to make me feel that way before. I was usually able to control myself, but I was really going overboard that night.

Then this man started moaning, "I want you. I want you."

There's a clear separation between dancing and getting aroused that a professional stripper needs to learn how to navigate, but every once a while, somebody can catch you off guard, and that was my night for it.

With all of the moaning and shit that this man was doing—as if we were fucking—one of the security guys peeked through the curtains to make sure everything was still professional and had not crossed the line.

"Are you okay?" the guard asked me.

Shit, I was about to make my money *and* get good and wet, so I winked my eye at the security and nodded. "I'm fine. I got this."

He closed the curtain back and left us alone. All the while, I kept tabs on how many songs were being played so I could charge his ass accordingly. He had already paid three-hundred for our private room, but after about eight songs and thirty minutes, my personal tab was already up to five-hundred.

I was straight honest about it and on business, so I told the man to make sure he wouldn't be shocked by it and trip out on me. And whether he knew it or not, his ass was ready to pay my bills that night.

After I told his tab, he paused and stood up to think about it to make sure he wanted to continue. With his dick still hard in his pants, he handled me six-hundred dollars.

Halleluyah! I thought to myself. I needed that money. But then he started moving real slow, like he didn't really want to leave. I could tell how bad he wanted me.

The next thing I knew, he stopped and said, "Wait a minute." He pulled out another stack of hundred-dollar bills as if he had just come from the bank and propositioned me with it.

He said, "I want you right here and right now, and you can have all of this money in my hand."

It had to be at least fifteen-hundred dollars in his hand if not *more*. Well, shit, I was *game*. I wasn't a hoe, but I needed the money. That's what I was in the strip club to do, and money made a bitch *move* in the club—even me.

Now, when he said that he *wanted* me like that, I knew he meant more than a lap dance, so I had to be prepared for whatever. And I actually stood there in this private room behind a curtain and allowed this man to strip me ass, butt-naked, like a baby, and sit on his lap with his big, hard dick was throbbing. I felt like I had a date with a freaky-ass Santa Claus, but what else was I supposed to do? He had already showed me the money.

When I first started stripping at the clubs, I wouldn't have done no shit that like no matter *how* much money a man would offer me. But after my third year in the game, I remembered madam Cocoa from The A, who told me "a real bitch will do what she needs to do." And I had been around my girl Diamond long enough to realize that shit in action. Nor was I a new bitch in the game anymore. So I was ready to take it to that next level if I had to. But at least I wasn't all out in the open with it. I was still behind a VIP curtain with nothing on but my boots.

This man asked me, "Are you okay?" to make sure that I wouldn't trip out on him.

"Yeah, I'm okay." I was a big fucking girl, with a big girl's decision to make. I asked him, "So, what's up?" What did he want me to do for the money and that big dick of his?

He pulled out a gold Magnum condom from his pocket as if he had come ready for something extra that night and he knew that he would get it. "I won't you to go down on it."

What the *fuck*? That nigga wanted me to suck his dick in the club, behind the VIP curtains for a few thousand dollars to pay my damn bills. And you know what... I took the fucking condom from his huge hands to do it, while praying that the security guard wouldn't look back into the curtains to check in on me.

I said, "You can't make a lot of noise though." I didn't want his ass back there again moaning and shit.

He smiled and whispered, "I promise I won't," before he handed me the money.

That's how the grown men were. They weren't about that bullshit, like some of the younger guys. I probably still wouldn't have tried that shit with a twenty-something. But this older man seemed like the type who didn't do a lot strip clubs. He just had that feeling for me that night, and he had hit the jackpot with his money.

I opened up his pants and pulled out his big, long and hard dick. It was standing up tall like a baseball bat. He was already wet and slippery around his head with anticipation. Then I opened up the condom and slid it down on him, holding it steady with my fingers to make sure I guided it into my mouth without choking.

While on my knees inside this VIP room in the strip club, it didn't matter how popular or flashy I was, or how much money I had made in the past, I was still in the moment and needed to get that paper. The thin line between prostitution and stripping is a real part of the business that will never change. Any bitch who would tell you anything differently is *lying*. No motherfucker is his right *mind* is gonna keep giving girls money only to dance for him. But it's up to *you* to decide whether you wanna take it to that next level or not. Every dancer, stripper, entertain or whatever is gonna be propositioned to do *more* by serious men with money in their hands. Even a few *women* will come at you sometimes.

So I sucked this man's dick inside the room for money, while hoping to *God* that I didn't get caught in there. And as I sucked up and down on his big, hard dick, he leaned back into the comfortable sofa and continued to moan, "Oh, baby, oh, baby," as he pumped his hips slowly into my.

With no time to waste, I wanted to make sure I did it good enough to make him come fast—the faster the better. I didn't even complain when he grabbed me by the back of my head and long hair to push me down into him.

His big dick was so wide in my mouth that it stretched my lips.

"Yeah, baby, suck my dick. Suck my dick," he whispered to me.

I looked up in his eyes like a nasty little girl as I continued to work my lips and tongue up, down and around his dick. "Yes, daddy. Is that how you like it?" I whispered back.

I just wanted him to hurry up and come fast before I got caught. When he started jerking and bust a nut, I could feel the veins in his dick, throbbing in my mouth as he squirted his semen into the condom. I had made this man come in four minutes and was happy that the condom didn't break. A four-minute song was all it took and it was over with. My dick-sucking game was that good. And before anyone knew it, he had done his business and I had done mine.

Thinking back to it, I even can't lie. Even though I was able to get the money I needed that night, that shit turned me off from KODs. The Uno didn't even have any private rooms to do no shit like that. So I started going back to The Uno and Primadonna's again. Even though he had given me his number, I didn't want to come face to face with this older man at KODs again after that VIP-room experience. I felt embarrassed by what I had done, and I would rather act like it had never happened.

I was forced to think about that VIP-room experience a lot. Despite my high and mighty first few years of dancing with my nose all up in the air, the strip club life had pulled me down to sucking dick for money, like any other common hoe in the street. Of course, I didn't go around bragging about it like Coco or some other girls did, but how could I *ever* to talk about them anymore? I had been pulled back down to the bottom like anyone else.

That shit at KODs made my return to The Uno feel like a homecoming. I now knew that the low-key spot in Little Haiti had the best of what the strip club life had to offer me. The Uno was like Miami's version of the TV show *Cheers*, where you just felt comfortable and familiar. And sure, Big Pete had a gang of dancers that he was fucking, and Moist was a pain in the ass sometimes, but they somehow managed to run that club like a joint a money-making joint in Las Vegas.

Looking back at it, none of us dancers ever really wanted to leave The Uno. The environment was on point, safe and top-notch for girls to make good money there. Big Pete had gone out of his way to network and push hard to bring celebrities and regular clientele into the club for the dancers to dance for and make their cake. But shit happens and things change. That's just how life goes. Nothing remains the same forever, especially something as volatile as the strip club life.

After years of running the club with no hick-ups, Big Pete and the property owner were both arrested for a on a six-hundred-thousand dollar tax theft charge. The fucked up thing about it was that he property owner, an old white woman who had inherited the club from her murdered husband years ago, had never even been down to the club. I don't even know if that old woman knew what the hell was going on. Or maybe she did and didn't know the extent of it. Apparently, Big Pete had been charging all of the customers taxes without giving the money back to the state of Florida and they had finally come after him for it, taking the owner down with him.

We were hearing all kinds of conflicting stories about what was going on, but Big Pete had been running The Uno for *years* without this older white woman being involved or in the way, until Don came along to help him run it.

Don was this older, short white guy from Boston, who many people said was an undercover cop, placed there by the IRS to help take The Uno down. But this old, white-woman owner had fallen for the okie doke by allowing him into the club to help run it with Big Pete. I don't know where she knew Don from, or who talked her into trusting him, or if he knew her late husband or whatever, but when this white came to work there, it was the beginning of the end.

Out of nowhere, everyone showed up to start work at The Uno one morning and discovered a large padlock with big chains across the door. This white woman owner had just shut the place down. I don't know what was on her mind or what she was angry about, but she was showing everyone that she was still in control of the property. In fact, she pulled up in the parking lot in her car black BMW and stood out there with her crew and locksmith right as Big Pete arrived in his plush, white Range Rover. He usually showed up early to pick up the money.

He looked around and asked the owner right out in front of us, "What's going on?"

We had day shift dancers, security, bartenders and even some customers had pulled up early to see what was going on. But the owner wasn't hearing it. I didn't know what her beef was, but something had seriously pissed her off that morning.

She told him, "Pete, I trusted you!" as if he had stolen money from her or whatever. But you could tell that she didn't want to go in to it out in the open like that.

But Pete went off. He said, "I've been running this club for *years*! You don't know anything about this business. I've made *plenty* of money for you and this how you repay me, with *this*?"

It was tense and depressing out there to see Big Pete locked out the club like that. He was the Boss as far as we knew, so to have a small, old white woman to pop up like that and shut him down was crazy. It was like another *King Kong* in New York movie, and the black beast was being killed by the white woman again.

We were all standing there in shock, wondering what Big Pete would do next, but business is business and fights over money always shut shit down. Evidently, the money wasn't adding up right, so the owner had shown her cards. All I knew was that The Uno was how a lot of people made their living and paid their bills. That easy dancing money had provided for people's families and had helped a lot of them out of some tough situations, including me and my family. So of course, I was angry as hell about that. I didn't want to deal with a lot of the other clubs. I was tired of having to fly down to the Virgin Islands to earn less money and I still had bills to pay and a life to provide for.

The Uno shut down for a week to straighten out the club's new direction or whatever, and the owner placed Don back in to manage. At that point, I started thinking about dancing at Primadonna's, the other get-money strip club for black girls in Miami. In the meantime, I was getting small money at CoCo's in Lake Side, where I first saw my sister Naomi dancing. CoCo's was worse than Dimes Chicks in Miami Gardens, but at least I didn't have to worry about fighting no bitches in there, because the girls already knew me and wouldn't fuck with me. They guys in there knew me too.

144

But there were so many pimps and lustful niggas walking in and out of CoCo's that these girls became a lot more desperate to get their money. The guys in were more into a girl stripping butt-ass naked than dancing, and they would tell you that upfront too. They dancers were not top of the line anyway, with their dress code, their overall professional style *or* their hygiene. You know, if you want to get top money you have make yourself worth it.

Well, The Uno and Primadonna's were the top spots, so until The Uno could get its act together, I had to go back over to Primadonna's to start making my new money over there again. Fuck it, the money and the strip club life was still calling me. And like, Mary J. Blige, I felt that I was going down for it.

Cisco

I first met this guy named Cisco when he had walked into my territory at The Uno. He was new meat in the club I had just come back from making money down in the Virgin Islands again, and I needed a new man. It was something about losing Trini like I did in St. Thomas that made me yearn for a new relationship. I was just ready to settle my ass down with somebody for a minute. Otherwise, I would have stuck to my rules of not dealing with strip club niggas and left this new guy alone.

But when I first set eyes on Cisco—with people already talking about him inside the club—I saw that he had a long scar across his face as if he had smashed him with a bottle. I guess I was still a sucker for a man with a hard-life story to tell, because his hood nigga looks turned me the hell on. I can't even lie. But he still had class about himself.

Through my earlier experiences with hardened men, I thought that I could see right through his grimy look and get to the heart of his emotions. He was a Haitian man with a big ego and neatly done dreadlocks and no accent. So I began to stare at this new man from the top of the stage as he stared at me.

As I caressed my body with my hands and got ready to walk out on stage to dance, I could just feel it in my bones that he was going to be my new nigga. So I fondled my titties and bent over to show my ass to make sure that Cisco could see my whole package before I even walked out. I was wearing five-inch, golden leather, thigh-high boots and just knew that I was the shit that night. I was ready to kill it right in this man's thugging-ass face. But I continued to observe him from head to toe, because I wasn't fucking with no scrubs—not after losing Trini in the islands. My taste buds in a man had definitely gone up.

Cisco was wearing a pair of black, True Religion jean, a long-sleeve black T-shirt and black leather Prada sneakers. He was also blinged out in a diamond chain and big-faced, Frank Mueller watch. That shit was so bright and sexy in the dark with shining lights that it make my pussy wet from just staring at it, because I knew that Cisco had exquisite taste like mine.

I got so excited that I returned to the dressing room to toss on the right smell good on, knowing that I wanted to get up close and personal with this nigga. And when I came back out to take the stage, he was still sitting there waiting on me like I knew he would be. So I did my thing onstage and front him and thanked him for the money that he threw on me. It was all a part of my slow but sure enticement of his ass.

So I buttered him up with just enough small talk to get him to spend some more money on me. "I like your style. You got that look tonight."

He grinned like a crook and said, "Yeah, I like your look too. Would you like a drink?"

Hell yeah! I thought to myself. But I could never show it and come off too eager. I had to keep is sassy and classy.

So I told him calmly, "Yeah, I'm drinking. And I'll have Moet."

When he paused, I began to hope that his ass wasn't cheap and on a budget. I couldn't stand for a budget nigga in my life. You had to be about it for real and not just role playing.

He asked me, "Are you just drinking that because I'm buying it?"

"No, I'm drink it because that's what I *like* … and I can *afford it*," I told him with a slight attitude. If that nigga couldn't deal with my expensive taste, then he needed to move on.

Cisco smiled and wasn't fazed by it. That's when I knew I had him. My game was way tighter than the petty bitches who only worked at The Uno. I had experienced that next level shit and wasn't trying to come back down. I had figured out how to get into a nigga's mind and his pockets.

Cisco ordered the bottle of Moet and handed it to me, while he got a glass a Remi and Red Bull with ice for himself. Then we reintroduced ourselves like Jay Z song.

He asked me if I wanted to dance for him, but not a lap dance. He said he didn't want me all over his nice jeans like some hard-dick sucker. It was all good with me, as long as I still got paid.

Before I could finish my dance, he had to take a phone call and handed me fifty dollars before he left the room. The nigga even had the nerve to tell me to wait there for him until I got back.

Shit, not for fifty fucking dollars! I thought to myself as he walked out.

I already knew what it was with the hustlers in Miami. They were money chasers. Every phone call was about that money, but as bad as I wanted his ass, I wasn't waiting on him for a couple of dollars. I had already made a G by ten o'clock, so I was ready to keep it moving as usual. Besides, those fancy-ass tall boots of mine were burning my damn feet up and I had to get my ass up out them things.

By the time I walked out of the front door to leave, Cisco was just about to walk back in and was mad at me because I was leaving.

"I thought I told you to wait for me," he said with an attitude of his own. That's a confident nigga for you.

They were all selfish that way. If not, then they must have not been able to get it. But I also knew that when a real nigga wants you, he won't let you leave easily either.

So I laughed and said, "I already made what I needed to for tonight so I'm going home." And I walked over to my brand new, metallic, G35 Infiniti Coupe.

"Damn, so you're *leaving*? You can't wait for me."

I could tell that Cisco was another one of the spoiled-ass guys who always got his way or acted like a bitch when he couldn't. But it was much better for a nigga to miss you than to get tired of you, so it was best that I left his ass early. Maybe next time he would understand how important my time and my money was.

So I told his ass, "Maybe I'll stay next time," and took my ass to my car.

I returned to The Uno that Thursday night and was surprised to see Cisco there. I thought maybe it would take at least a few more days before he would pop up again, but so be it. However, Cisco wasn't surprised to see me. Evidently he had been clocking for me to return.

He even told me, "I wasn't planning on speaking to your ass again because you left me that night I told you not to."

I was like, *What the fuck?* He really showing feelings for me and didn't even realize it. He sounded like girl with her heart broken. That made me turn my shit on him stronger.

So when I danced for him that night, I made sure to shoves my ass all up in his lap and sat on his hard dick, whether he wanted me to or not, because I knew that I could have my way with him. The nigga had shown me his emotional cards too fast. But I actually didn't mind that. I'd rather have an emotional man who I could get a rise out of then one of those ice-cold guys who calculated everything. What fun was that?

Well, the feeling was mutual. I obviously turned

Cisco on as much as he turned me on. I needed a little emotional foreplay with my man. So we traded phone numbers that night and he told me that he wanted to see me after I got off. But my damn phone kept going dead, so I couldn't charge it back up until I got over to my grandmother's house on my father's side, where I was staying at the time.

As soon as I charged my phone back up, my cell rang and it was Cisco calling me already.

He said, "You left *again*? I thought I told you I wanted to see you tonight."

That nigga was so pressed, but I thought the shit was sincere, so I started smiling. I told him, "My grandmother lives right around the corner, so calm down. I had to charge up this cheap-ass phone I have again. I really need to get a new one."

He said, "Okay, so you still trying to see me tonight?"

I said, "Yeah, give me like thirty minutes." I wanted to take my ass in the shower first because I knew I was ready to give him some pussy that night. So I got dressed and sped over to the address in Little Haiti where he texted me to meet him and found him in a silver Toyota Corolla.

That shit threw me for a loop. After meeting him in his diamonds and all of that other designer shit he wore, he couldn't afford nothing more than a low-budget Toyota? I figured he should have at least had a better car than mine. But I blew it off and didn't say anything about it.

Cisco got into my car, smelling *good*, wearing YSL cologne that made me want to suck his dick right there in the seats. He told me to drive to Wet Willy's on South Beach. We went inside and sat on a top-floor balcony drinking Sex On The Beach and Call a Cab.

Cisco wasted no time asking me some important

questions about my goals business-wise and with my finances. That caught me off guard too, because no man had ever asked me those kinds of questions before, not even my father. Sure, my father told me to have goals and a plan, but he didn't ask or teach me anything about business or finances. I don't think most guys even cared about how I dealt with my money. So that question had my head wide open for what Cisco had to say about it.

I told him about referrals and promotions down in the Virgin Islands at the Island Cove, and he was really feeling me and my independent hustle. He said most girls wouldn't have done anything like that even if they had the opportunity. In fact, a lot of guys wouldn't have done it.

He told me, "A lot of people don't really take advantage of real business opportunities unless it comes easily, but most good business doesn't come that easy."

I got nice and relaxed with him. Cisco was the first guy I could feel that serious about telling my personal business to. I usually didn't talk about business or money with guys at all—outside of getting money from them for dancing.

He started telling me how I could incorporate my promotions business and make it all legit with a brand name, a bank account and with taxes. Well, *damn*, that made me feel *real* special. Ain't nothing better in this *world* than a bitch having her own legitimate business to earn from. That made me feel like Cisco really wanted to see me win.

He then asked me how much money I wanted to make that upcoming year in 2011. This was around November 2010 after I had first met him.

I didn't have an exact number, so I just said, "A lot."

He said, "You gotta put a number on it to make it a real goal. Like, I want to make two-hundred and fifty thousand this year."

I smiled and said, "Me too."

Cisco turned up his face as if I wasn't taking it seriously enough, but I was. I just never had anyone to talk to about real goals like that before. Most people I was around only thought short term, like next week or next month, and usually had small goals to pay off some debt that they had.

Anyway, to make two-hundred and fifty thousand dollars in a year, Cisco must have been into some serious shit, and I was determined to find out what it was. He had me intrigued on more than just the personal level. I was thinking about making money on a much larger hustle without having to getting naked, but first I had to find out what that was.

I ended up over at Cisco condo that night in Miramar and we both were tipsy with liquor in our system, so you know what that meant. We was about to be some serious fucking going down. And we wasted no time getting into it as we started kissing aggressively.

Cisco open up my shirt and attacked my titties with his tongue, sucking and licking and fingering my nipples until they were hard and erect like sweet brown chocolate Hersey's kisses. My panties were as wet as the beaches in Miami and he had me ready to come before even taking his dick out. So I pulled out his big black dark from his pants and began to lick around the tip with my lips and tongue, while holding his cock tightly in my hands.

I could tell Cisco was enjoying it. He started moaning, "Oh, shit! Oh, shit!" and pushed my head down deeper to get all of it.

I didn't mind. I wanted to please Cisco that night and show him how much I appreciated him, so I tried my best to suck all of the energy out of him. He couldn't take my head game, with his body, jerking, squirming, twisted and cramping up.

"Keisha! Oh, Keisha! I love it, baby!" he screamed,

calling out my real name.

We wanted each other badly that night, so I pull Cisco on top of me on his bed and pulled on a condom to let him push his good dick deep inside my wet pussy, with my juices flowing all over him. I was so hot and freaky for him that night that I pulled his dick back out and licked my own shit off his condom covered dick as he stared into my eyes in disbelief.

But I wasn't just horny for his dick that night; I was scheming on a come-up and eager to find out what his hustle was. I was that determined to turn his ass out and gain his trust to get in on it. So I pushed his dick back into my wet, juicy pussy and let him fuck me crazy until we both came like two, drunken freaks.

After we were exhausted and resting in cum and sweat, Cisco got up to wipe my body off with a towel. Then he pulled me up and led me to the bathroom to take a full shower with him. No man had ever done that with me before either. So we climbed into the shower together and washed our bodies down with soap and bubbles and got horny again, fucking right there inside the shower as the warm water came down and washed us both off.

When I woke up that next morning, I was surprised to be wrapped up in Cisco's arms like a stuffed Teddy Bear. This man made me so damn special that I just *knew* that I had found my soul mate. So I spent the entire day with him until I had to go back to work at The Uno the next evening.

Cisco asked to borrow my car and to drop me off at work at The Uno, while he made his runs. He told me that he didn't have any cars of his in Miami and that he was renting cars. Now, I usually only let my family members use my cars, but I felt that I could trust Cisco, and I wanted him to trust me right back. So I allowed him to use my car after dropping me off.

Cisco came back to the club that night before I got

off and was entertained by a dancer named Tiny. But I didn't trip. Tiny was an OG, madam dancer, who still looked pretty good for her age. A lot of people said that she was the shit back in days of the Big Meech and the Black Mafia Family era back in the days in Atlanta. But she wasn't a threat to me in my era. It was my time now, so there was nothing for me to be concerned about with Tiny. She had already seen her better days at the clubs and she wasn't getting them back or getting any younger.

Well, when I walked back into the dressing room to freshen up and change clothes, Tiny followed me in and began to ask me questions about Cisco.

She was like, "You know Cisco? Where do you know him from? Are you fucking him?"

I wasn't trying to go there with this woman, so I told her, "You go take that shit up with him. I just met the man."

The next thing I knew, this woman Tiny started telling me how she and Cisco were fucking just the other day and she started calling him all kinds of pussy names and shit. But I kept my cool about it. I wanted no parts of that drama with her. I considered it all beneath me. I still had to hear the truth and get down to the bottom of things though.

With all of her rants, I already knew they had some history together. But fuck their past! As far as I was concerned, Cisco was my new property nigga, especially while he was driving around the city in my brand new Infiniti Coupe.

So when Tiny went screaming out of the dressing room to make her money for the night, I called Cisco's back there to ask him all about her.

"Do you know Tiny?" I asked him point blank.

He said, "Yeah." But he denied having any sexy relations with her in a *while*.

I said, "Well, she didn't act like it's been awhile. She

was just in here calling you all kinds of bitch niggas, pussies and everything, like you just had a hot dick a on the grill for her."

I was letting Cisco know that I was not some young dumb bitch that he could run any kind of game on, but at the same time, I let that shit slide because I didn't want anything from getting in the way of what I had in store for Cisco and me. And he liked the way I handled it without losing my cool and acting crazy about the shit.

That incident early on in our new relationship made Cisco trust and respect me even more. I had no choice but to keep my poise, while looking at him as a possible way out of the strip club life. We started dating officially and in a matter of weeks, we became inseparable. We went everywhere and did everything together. I even moved in with him, which was a giant step for me. I loved having my own space from the day I moved out of my momma's house. But I had bounced around a lot to keep from paying a waste of rent on places, while traveling to the Virgin Islands and moving around a lot.

Cisco and I moved into a two-bedroom, two-bath townhouse in North Miami. He really became my dream mate, cooking me breakfast every morning and bringing it to me in bed. I finally had my own man again and was not sharing him. Everything was going great with Cisco, or maybe I was in denial.

He kept asking me to send out gifts and toys to different locations saying they were for his daughters or his niece. But this one time when I didn't send a package overnight, Cisco started calling me out my name with the "dumb bitches" and "you ain't shit" talk that my father's girlfriend/wife used to pull when I was little.

I still didn't trip out on Cisco at that time, but I did think about his reactions and behavior was bazaar. He would say that I couldn't follow directions and all of that shit, while he would stay out for days and didn't allow me to question him about anything that he was doing. Our relationship had slipped into that questionable bullshit, where I started to think that maybe I was a dumb bitch who couldn't follow directions.

That's how shit goes when you let your guard down, you get punched right in your face while wondering what the fuck just happened. Overnight, I went from being confident and independent to doubting myself and wondering if I ever deserved a good man. I started thinking that I was a dumb bitch who couldn't get her life together, and I still thinking occasionally about Trini in the Virgin Islands. I wondered if I had made the wrong decision to leave him or if he would have started treating me badly too. I wasn't sure of anything anymore.

Then I started to question Cisco about all of these damn gifts and packages that he kept telling me to send out. I never checked inside of them to see what they were, but that shit became a way out of hand to me. Why the fuck did he have *me* doing all of that shit instead of him? I felt like a damn *servant*, like his personal concierge or some shit.

So I asked, "Cisco, what's up with all of these damn *toys*? I think all this shit is a little excessive, especially with you getting mad at me because I miss the delivery by a day or two. Do these kids have to have these toys like the next day? And how many daughters and nieces do you have?"

After awhile, that shit just didn't add up. The more I thought about it, the more it didn't make any sense to me. I didn't even see him buying any damn toys or wrapping them up, and he surely didn't ask me to do it. He would just hand me the packages already ready to go. So I was no longer going for that shit until he told me what the fuck was going on.

Finally Cisco broke down and told me the truth that there was something more inside of those packages.

Well, I was pissed. I knew *exactly* what the hell it

was, and that nigga could have gotten me arrested without even having a *clue* as to what was going on. I would have looked like a fucking idiot at the Post Office. Not only that, but all of the talk about Cisco helping me to develop my promotions business hit the back burner. He wasn't helping me at all. Everything was suddenly about his ass, and he was not treating the way we started off at all. It was just more bullshit from a selfish-ass man!

I had been holding the peace and anticipating him helping with my business for *months* and had not tripped on that nigga. I had turned into his sexy little puppet, just like he wanted me to. But that was *it*. I stopped mailing out Cisco's fucking packages and reached out to the owner of Primadonna's named Pop to ask him if I could establish my own promotions night in his club. I had a new itch for business that I wanted to scratch and it was time to stop waiting around for nothing and make it happen.

By that time, the business and clientele at The Uno had gone down without Big Pete running it anymore. The new white manager named, Don, was not as business savvy and didn't know what he was doing. He didn't really care about the business like that and he was allowing bitches to fight again and do whatever they wanted to do without tight rules. And the black customer didn't really trust his ass. He wasn't really one of us and he wasn't really cool either. So I wanted to try my new business at Primadonna's instead.

Primadonna's had a couple of nights that were not hot like that, so Cisco and I met up with the manger there named Pops and told him my ideas to host a slow club night and turn it into Porn Star Wednesdays, and the manager back with some crazy-ass bar guarantee of five-thousand dollars.

Cisco and I were like, "What? Dude, this is a slow-ass night. Why would we pay you that much for a bar guarantee when there's nobody even in the club that night?"

He must have thought we were desperate for it. So we left his ass alone to think about it. I figured I had the right vision for the club promotions game and Cisco owed me, so I talked his ass into helping me finance it and everything if he needed to. I had helped his ass, and he could have gotten me fucking arrested. So it was now time for him to help me out with something that was actually legal, especially after him talking all of that shot to me about my business and finances. It was time for that nigga to put his money where his mouth was, and I wasn't letting him off the hook either.

So Cisco agreed to it, and Pops called us back like a week later to renegotiate for only a five-hundred dollar bar guarantee that was more like it. We then planned a grand opening to kick-off after my twenty-fourth birthday on February 7, 2010, with an opening on that Wednesday night of the 9th, hosted by the porn star named Pinky. And I branded my first promotions night in Miami as Dior's World Entertainment, an entertainment and promotions company.

But the anticipation of my first big event didn't go smoothly at all, especially not with Cisco. Like a week before my big birthday and business come-out party, I caught his ass in the car with another stripper. Well, this time, I flipped the fuck out. We were too close to doing something *big* for his ass to act out like that so close to the grand opening. But he didn't pay me any mind, while attending more to this girl. And with the way he was treating her, all gently and shit, I assumed that they had just finished fucking.

I was all up in his face, screaming, "What the fuck is on your mind? Why would you do that shit?"

I mean, we were so *close* to being great business partners, and this nigga pulled up right in my face with another bitch like it's *nothing*. Evidently, he didn't give a fuck. I was pulling up to the condo and he was pulling out in a dark blue SL500 Benz that he had bought.

Adding insult to injury, the motherfucker slapped me right in my face out in front of a small crowd of people out there. I was so fucking hurt and humiliated. You can't even *imagine* the pain that I felt inside at that moment. Cisco was treating me like *trash*, even though I could have helped to bring him legal money instead of the crazy-ass, Post Office, drug shipping business that he was running.

I jumped in my car and drove back home to North Miami, devastated, while crying uncontrollably and feeling confused about what I wanted to do next. I still had my first big business night set-up to prepare for with this nigga. But he didn't even come home for the next few days. It was a good thing that he didn't too, because I was damn near ready to scheme out a way to kill his ass. That's how fucked up in the head I was. And I was too embarrassed to even call and talk to anyone about it, because they all knew me as strong-ass Keisha, who didn't break down for no one.

After two days of no communication with him, Cisco started calling me up and pleading with me, trying to reconcile the matter.

He was like, "I didn't mean that shit, Keisha. I was just caught up in the moment and embarrassed that you had caught me out there like that. And I couldn't go out like no *sucker* when you started tripping I me. You just caught me off guard that night, but I didn't mean to hit you like that. I was just a thoughtless reaction."

Do you believe that shit? And in my present state of mind, it all made sense to me. I did act out of character on him that night by screaming and acting out in public. That wasn't even my normal style. But I felt so disrespected that he would do something like that so close to my first big business night in the Miami promotions business.

My ass actually apologized to Cisco for blowing up

on him like that. I had been caught up in the moment as well. But I really loved him and wanted to work things out with him. I also realized that my business plans at Primadonna's was much more important than some jump-off bitch he had in the car.

He told me he didn't even fuck her, but I definitely didn't believe that shit. If he hadn't fucked her when I saw him with her, he surely fucked her over the next two days of not being home. Why wouldn't he fuck the bitch after already being caught with her? And since he hadn't come home, I figured that was automatic. He probably fucked her good both nights.

But ultimately, I didn't give a fuck. This man had money to start my new business with, so when he came back and we reconciled the bullshit, that's just what I told myself to focus on—Dior's World Entertainment.

Dior's World Entertainment

We were still on for my big birthday event a Primadonna's, hosted by Pinky The Porn Star, and everyone was talking about it. At the time, I didn't even know Pinky; I just knew that she was very popular porno star, who was in high demand in Miami. I called up her booking agency to get her to host my event, and the fee was thirty-five-hundred dollars for her flight from Atlanta, the hotel and everything. Including Pinky's fee, the entire event cost about forty-five-hundred dollars, with the marketing fliers, security and decorations. So I was very excited about my first promotional event and was ready to put up with all of Cisco's bullshit to pull it off together, but I was really thinking about establishing my own shit one day.

For my birthday party bash, I had Primadonna's fully decorated with silk white drapes, hanging from the ceiling. I ordered over a hundred pink and white balloons with my name Dior spelled out in big, bold letters, all floating up to the ceiling with pink and black ribbons. It was beautiful. I even had my dance costume custom made with pink and black lacing and my name embroidered across the back.

After making sure that everything was set just right, I looked like a million bucks the night of my first big party. I showed up early on business mode to get everything just right in the back, and it was a packed-ass party as soon as I walked in. I wasn't even ready yet, so I had to stay out of sight for awhile. People had driven in from everywhere and were all giving me respect, walking up to greet me and congratulate me on pulling off my big night.

Then the DJ called my name from the booth to hit the front stage.

"*Dee-orr!* It's your night, baby girl. Everyone give it up for Dior's World Entertainment."

As I approached the front stage to make my grand appearance for the crowd, people saw me walking as money started flying from every direction. We even had Rico Love up in the building with all of the big spenders. Rico Love was a big-time R&B music producer for Beyonce, Usher, Chris Brown, Kelly Rowland, P. Diddy and more. And he spent a lot of money on me to make it rain that night too. It was all crazy and fun to be a part of.

As the DJ continued to yell out my name and tell the people to keep spending their money and make it rain for my birthday, you couldn't even walk on the floor in there without stepping on green dollar bills. As we say in the strip clubs, the green carpet was *everywhere*. I was even slipping on money as I tried to walk. So the club manager had to call someone to the stage to sweep the money off with a broom.

Once we stacked it all up in big black garbage bags, we counted eight-thousand dollars that night from the dance floor and my performances alone. Then I pulled another five thousand from splitting the door money with Cisco for thirteen thousand dollars.

This is what the fuck I'm talking about! I told myself. That was the kind of money I was trying to make *every* night. But with thirteen-thousand dollars from just one event, I wouldn't have to grind as hard to get it anymore. Thirteen Gs in one night was real hustling.

I walked backstage, where I had a VIP area set up for Pinky The Porn Star, who was loud, drinking and having a good time with her manger Danielle and friends. We had porn star Gazelle Triple X in the house too and a good friend of mine named Patrick. And they were all treating me good on my first big night.

I said, "Hey, y'all," and greeted everyone inside the room, giving Patrick a hug.

Patrick was like *family* to me. I had known him for several years and we had always been nothing but friends. Patrick was light skin with slick, dark hair, like the mixed look of Jamaican Cooleys. He was a pretty boy to most women, but he still wasn't my type, so I had never gone for him like that. He was just good people.

Cisco had been pretty quiet for most the night, while eyeballing all of the money that I was making in there. But suddenly he wanted to call me over and talk to me from the VIP area.

I walked over to Cisco, smiling and feeling good about our successful night. I asked him, "What's up, babe?" I figured it was something small.

But Cisco goes off on me. "What the fuck you doing hugging up on some nigga?"

Now this is the same man who smacked me in my face after I had caught him out there with some bitch in his car, and he hauled off and slapped me for it. But and I had done was hugged an old friend at my birthday party.

Before I could say anything to explain who Patrick was, Cisco swung a punch straight to my stomach and knocked the wind out of me. In pain and shock, I crumpled to the floor and tried to catch my breath. I couldn't believe that he had punched me in my stomach at my big party in front of all of those people. I mean, it was a huge crowd.

You could hear the silence as the people watched but didn't move to do anything, not even the security guards. Cisco had that kind of pull in Miami. People knew who he was and didn't want to fuck with him.

Embarrassed and sobbing, as soon as I caught my breath, I quickly climbed to my feet and went to gather all of my things to leave. That motherfucker had ruined my party and I no longer wanted to be there. So I left as fast as I could without even saying good bye to everyone.

I mean, how could a nigga be that damn *evil* and *selfish* on my big night like that?

To top it off, when Cisco arrived at home that night, he was still beefing with me. He was yelling, "You fucking embarrassing me in there, hugging up on some nigga."

I said calmly, "Cisco, Pat is like *family*. You've met Pat several times before." Cisco just didn't pay attention to anything but what *he* wanted to do. He probably was also insecure about Patrick looking so good, but he had nothing to e concerned about from me. Like I said, Patrick was only a friend.

He said, "I don't give a fuck if I met him before; you don't hug up on no nigga in front of me. The fuck are you *thinking*?" he yelled. "I helped to you *pay* for this shit and put it all together, and that's how you do me?"

I said, "But Cisco, we both made good *money* tonight."

"That ain't no fucking money," he snapped at me. "That's *small* shit. I make that in my *sleep*."

That was what the real issue, *I* believe. Cisco was upset that I had done something on my own that had *worked*, and in his jealousy, we was trying to find a way to ruin it for me. Thirteen-thousand dollars in one night was good money for *anyone*. But this man showed no regrets at all about hitting me out in public in front of everyone—again. There was no emotions or thoughts about his actions toward me at all, and I was *tired* of it.

I told myself, *Girl, you gotta get yourself together and move on from this nigga before he really tries to hurt you one day.*

I thought that Cisco might try to *kill me* the next time. He was really unstable. But yet I *refused* to move on from him. I still loved the man and would do anything to prove it. That's how he got me to start delivering his packages out of town.

He said, "If you wanna make some *real* money, you would go on the *road* for me."

"Go on the road and do *what?*" I asked.

"Deliver these fucking packages."

I had always been around the dope game in Miami, but I had never really been *in it.* I still remember my brother Pat Pat being pissed off that I even saw his drug house. But when Cisco offered me five-hundred dollars just to make drop-off runs, I was intrigued by the how easy it could be.

"And all I need to do is drop off a package?"

"Drop it off, get the money and come back."

I immediately thought of calling him on the phone whenever I would make a drop off to pick up money. I didn't want him thinking that I would ever try to *steal* anything from him. I wanted everything to be on the up and up. So like a hungry hustler, I agreed to do it.

The next thing I knew, Cisco had me dropping off boxes to different cities two and three times a week. He had me driving all the way up North too—to New York, Washington DC, Newport News, Virginia, and to the Midwest in Missouri and Chicago. I was alone, nervous and inexperienced, but I kept thinking about the money and getting away from the strip club life. Making a few thousand dollars a week just to drive packages to different cities seemed like a piece of cake to me, as long as I drove the speed limit and didn't get pulled over by any cops out on the road.

But after awhile—with me delivering all of these packages with no incident—Cisco kept saying that he would pay me later. It got to the point where he owed me thousands of dollars, but since he was making that kind of money, I didn't sweat it. Cisco could have handed me five-thousand dollars whenever he got good and ready to. Then he started buying me all kinds of expensive gifts to cover up what he *really* owed me, like watches, gold bracelets, necklaces, expensive purses and shit like that. Sometimes the gifts would be worth thousands of dollars too, like when he bought me a Rolex. But it got to the point where he owed me *more* than his gifts were worth, and I needed my fucking *money*. After making several runs a week for about six months straight, this nigga owed me close to *eighteen-thousand* dollars! So I realized that he was using me and taking me for a *fool* because I loved him so much.

Sure, he would take care of my car note and phone bills and stuff like that, and since I lived with him, I didn't have to pay any rent. But I used to have my *own* cash money in my hands and giving my family money, so I wasn't having his *bullshit*. Business was business to me, no matter how much I loved a man.

I asked him, "Cisco, what's up with the money that you owe me for all my runs? I got *needs* and shit to for money like *you* got. And you know I'm not dancing like that anymore, while out on the road."

I mean, it was like this nigga was trying to keep me as broke slave. So I was trying to explain the obvious to him. I needed *cash* money like everyone else. That's when Cisco broke down and leveled with me. He wasn't really a major player in the dope game with the guys that he was dealing with. He was more like the delivery man, a fucking UPS service for drugs, and he still wasn't making that next level of money like I thought he was.

He said, "I'm just looking for that major deal to come through soon, so we have to stay consistent with this."

I understood what he meant. As a middle man in the dope game, you always have to *prove* that you're trustworthy enough for the big ballers to give you more product to make your money from. Or at least that's what he told *me*. But I didn't have time to wait around for that big hit shit. I still had shit to do with my money, including helping my sister Naomi out like I always did. I knew that there was money in the dope game was all around us. I saw Cisco pulling in sixty- and seventy-thousand dollars, and he couldn't tell me that all that money was just to flip more product. He just didn't want to share it with me.

After that first year, I felt more comfortable in the game to reach out to a few connects that I gotten to know over time to see what I could do to help out the process, because I was tired of hearing Cisco's excuses.

Through all of my friendships and contacts at the different strip clubs in Miami, I knew about *plenty* of people in the dope game, I just hadn't dealt with any of them. I didn't *need* to deal with them and I still didn't trust most of those people—especially the guys, who were always trying to fuck you. I didn't need that extra drama in my life while dealing with Cisco either. I already knew that he wouldn't be able to handle me dealing with baller guys, so I reached out to a few *female* connects in the game instead. It wasn't like women didn't know what was going on when their men, brothers and cousins. So many women had gotten into the dope game too.

This OG chick who first opened me up on the game was named Viola. She was a tall, Miami legend who knew everything there was to know about the streets *and* the dope game hustle. I knew her from the strip club life, and she sat me down and gave me so much knowledge I figured I couldn't *lose* with her.

In the meantime, I still needed my *money*, so I went back to stripping at night, while planning out my dope game during the day time. Whenever I wasn't traveling, I was plotting out my next move. I started planning a lot when I traveled too. I had a lot of time alone to think to myself while out on the road. So I started scheming on what I needed to do to make some real money in the dope game with all of the knowledge that Viola had dropped on me.

The first thing I did was let Cisco know that I wasn't making any more runs for him without getting paid. I understood that he wasn't making what he wanted to yet, but with the fifteen and twenty-thousand dollar payments that I was bringing back to him without touching it, he surely could pay my fucking *five-hundred*. You know? So he didn't have any *choice* but to pay me what he owed me at the *minimum*.

The OG Viola hooked me up with another female connect in Miami named Alberta. And this chick hustled harder than any man I ever saw.

She never told me her age, but I suspected she was in her mid- to late-thirties because of all she knew and what she liked to talk about. She always told me, "These niggas don't expect me, so I jump on them *quick* and run my shit *hard* and *fast*. You never know when these niggs wanna trip out on you because you're a *woman*."

So when she started dealing with Cisco, on account of me, she kept the shit strictly business with him, and he had to respect her. She was the one with the bigger money. But I was still doing most of the work, delivering the packages, collecting the money, taking it to the safe boxes—*everything*. Sometimes, when Cisco would be out of town, I had to coordinate everything with Alberta myself. And I never got paid for any of the extra work that I did. But I was learning shit, and that knowledge of the game was priceless.

We ended up dealing with this hustling-hard sister in Miami for *months*, and things were running smoothly with her, but Cisco was out of town too often to handle the day to day business, leaving more and more of it up to me. So as I continued to meet up and deal with Alberta, she began to trust me in the game. Or at least I *thought* she did.

I had to meet up with Alberta this one time, while the team owed her twenty-thousand dollars on a deal. I still considered myself just a delivery girl at the time, and I could feel the tension rising when I met up with her. She was holding a package for us, and we had given her fifteen thousand dollars in increments, and I was bringing her the final five thousand to finish the package.

You don't fuck with people's money in the dope game. They all play for *keeps* and the bullshit could mean your *life*! So when I pulled up to her location in Miami to meet her with the rest of the money, and she was acting mad funny and suspicious about everything. I knew it was about the money being broken up into parts instead of coming all at once. We gave her ten thousand, then five thousand and I had the last five. But Alberta was still irked by it.

She started yapping outside my car window in the parking lot where we met. "Come on, Dior. Give me the money."

I always thought this woman was wired a little too anxious. She reminded me of the tomboy chicks that I knew in high school, and the hardcore bitches who liked girls in the strip clubs. They always seemed a little overboard. And that day Alberta was in rare form. She was extra loud and acting out of character. So I didn't trust her. I was skeptical before I even drove out there that day, so I had Cisco to tell one his team members named Boston to drive out there to cover me.

They called this guy Boston because he was from way up North in Massachusetts. He was another tall, stocky guy, built like a handsome football player. But you could tell that he was from up North by how he carried himself. Boston was always in the cut, taking care of his business without being overly dramatic, like a lot of Miami guts were. And he was real cool to be around.

So I had Alberta's money on me and was ready to give it to her, but I didn't like how she was pushing all hard for it all out in the open like that. Then I spotted a blue Mazda was parked across the street from us with a guy who was just sitting there. I didn't trust that shit either. I wanted to do the handoff somewhere more private and safe. So I hesitated, feeling like it was a set up.

"All right, chill a minute. Calm down," I told her. I was still studying my surroundings, but Alberta wouldn't calm her hot ass down.

She said, "Look, do you have the money or not?"

Okay, is she trying to rob me or turn me into the police? I asked myself. *What the fuck is going on?*

You start thinking all kinds of shit in the dope game. That's why I told Cisco to have one of his guy's to follow me out there. I knew we owed Alberta the rest of her money and she wasn't happy about waiting. It's all about respect for people's money in the dope game. I wasn't new to that part.

"Let's ride and talk about it," I told her. I was still studying my surroundings and trying to figure her out. I didn't even want to tell her that I had the money on me. I was also waiting until I saw Cisco's guys pull up somewhere nearby to cover me. Once I saw Boston and them park near the bank across the street, I felt more confident.

"Come on, Alberta, let me talk to you in the car," I insisted.

I wasn't budging to give her the money until I felt more comfortable.

Finally, Alberta climbed in the car with me so I could drive around the block and talk her to see what was going on with this blue Mazda. That's when this car started to follow us. All the while, Alberta kept asking me about the money.

"Where's the fucking money, Dior?"

I was busy watching for the Mazda that started following behind us in my rearview mirror.

I said, "Who is this following us in this blue car?"

Alberta looked back and shook her head. "I don't

know. What are you talking about?"

She said it too fast and blew me off. I was sure it was a set-up after that. I didn't trust that shit at all. So I lied to her.

"Cisco has the rest of the money and he said he'll call you to make the drop off." I then saw Cisco's guys pulling up a couple of cars behind us. I was basically driving around the block in circles until I could decide what I wanted to do.

Alberta said, "Why are you bullshitting me, Dior? Where's the money?"

"I'm not bullshitting you. I told you, I don't *have* the money. Cisco told me to let you know that he'll call you."

She said, "He could have called and told me that shit himself."

I didn't tell her anything else until I rounded the corner and brought her back to her car in the parking lot—a silver Chrysler.

"All right, Cisco will call you." I was ready to get my ass out of there in a hurry. My heart was beating fast the whole time, but I knew what I needed to do.

Alberta asked me, "You sure he's gonna call me?" She climbed out of the car and didn't trust me either.

As soon as she shut the door back, I said, "Yeah, he'll call you," and I peeled my ass out of there.

Alberta started yelling at my car, "What are doing? *Dior?* Come back!"

I wasn't trying to hear that shit. Nor did I answer her calls when she started blowing up my cell phone. I just *knew* that I had just dodged a bullet. She was either trying to set me up for a robbery or me arrested by the police, so I left with the money and no package from her. And Cisco lost his fifteen-thousand dollars. But it was better than me getting robbed, killed or arrested on some crazy vendetta shit.

So I called his ass up and told him about it. "Man,

that bitch Alberta was trying to set me the fuck up. I *knew* something was funny."

Cisco said, "What are you talking about?"

"She kept talking about giving her the money all out in the open, and then someone started following us in a blue Mazda."

"What? Are you sure?"

"Hell *yeah*, I'm sure!" I yelled at him. "Ask your guys; they saw it. Ask Boston."

"So, did you give her the money?"

"No, and I didn't get the package either."

"Shit!" he cursed. "That's fifteen-thousand dollars!"

"Cisco, *fuck that*!" I yelled back. "I'm not going to *jail* or getting *killed* over some *bullshit*! Fuck that money! You give it to her yourself then." I meant it too. Cisco was still trying to use me to do his dirty work.

Cisco realized he was wrong. He said, "All right, fuck it. Damn!"

I didn't *care* if he was mad at me. I wasn't going back to that woman. I thought we were cooler than that at one point, but you just can't trust people in the dope game.

"Motherfucking *shit*!" I cursed myself. I had never been that scared in my *life*, and it all came out once I drove away. I couldn't even *breathe* behind the wheel. And it took me a long time to calm down.

Then I called Viola and told her about it to see what she thought.

She was like, "What? She did that?" She was *shocked* because she had hooked me up with the woman. She asked me, "Did Cisco fuck up her money?"

It was question I didn't have a good answer for. We did owe the woman her money.

Viola told me, "Baby girl, you can't fuck with her money like that. In this game, once you start with late debts and bad money deals, you can't go back to those people. They don't forget that shit."

I already knew it. That's why I didn't trust Alberta that day. I knew she was mad about us owing her late money, so she acted just like a villain in a drug movie.

Deep down inside, I knew that Cisco was a cheap ass, who was always trying to squeeze a dime out of a nickel and his bullshit wasn't adding up.

Even Viola told me, "Girl, don't let this man get you into some bullshit that you can't get yourself out of. You wanna be able make your own decisions. You hear me?"

"Yeah, I hear you." What the fuck else could say?

So that connection with Alberta was over with. I wasn't going back to her. Cisco had some other connections to deal with, but I didn't want to be involved in it anymore. I went back to focusing on stripping and promoting my own events. That's when Cisco begged to get involved in a much bigger deal.

"Dior, we could make *twenty-eight*-thousand dollars off this *one* package."

I said, "Well, you go get it then."

"You know I can't do that. Too many people know me."

"Yeah, so you'll have *me* to get locked up or killed," I responded. I was not doing it anymore. And little did he know—with the knowledge of the game that I had built up from OG Viola and being around it—I had saved up my money and bought a package of my own to move with some of Cisco's guys. Boston and them all knew me well enough at that point to trust me. So I had some of his crew to work the packages that I bought at the same time they were working Cisco's.

Its fuck up how things can get that way, but even Cisco's guys saw how he was constantly using me, and they all wanted to make more money. To make matters worse, they knew that I was more generous than Cisco, so Boston knew they could make more money with me. That caused a rift when Cisco found out. But instead of his getting mad at them for working with me, he tried to badmouth me in front of them.

He was like, "Why y'all fucking with Dior like that, B? She don't know what she doing? She don't even know how to buy the right shit."

They all knew about Cisco's bullshit by then. He was trying to say anything and everything to keep most of the money. He was always full of excuses as to why he couldn't pay anyone what they were worth. He even got into an argument with Boston, who had seen the blue Mazda following behind me that day with Alberta.

But Boston told him straight up, "You need to stop that shit, man. Dior is mad loyal, and you keep treating her like she's *not*. But she hasn't taken a *dime* from you while making all of your runs. That's shit looks like loyalty to me."

Boston's guys already knew how much product they had chopped up and how much money they had been moving with Cisco, so he couldn't even lie to them about shit.

Cisco got so mad about hearing the truth that they starting fighting and he ended up pulling out a gun on Boston. That's why petty and greedy he was. He would rather fight somebody then face up to the truth.

He yelled, "Nigga, don't you *ever* fucking disrespect me like that!"

It was a tense moment, but nobody moved. They knew that Cisco had a hot temper, but he didn't want to go to *jail* for murder over some petty shit. And his guys were *right*. He *was* discrediting me.

Boston said, "You know what? Fuck doing anymore business with you if you gon' act like that. That shit is plain *greedy*, man, so I can't get down with you no more."

Cisco was like, "Fuck you too then. I don't need to do business with y'all."

They didn't shoot each other—thank *God*—but was

pretty much it. Boston and his guys didn't do any more business with Cisco, and that left me stranded in the middle of it, because I had been dealing with all of them. But a lot of people didn't trust Cisco anymore. So it was only a matter of *time* before he lost everyone he had been dealing with. Or at least *I* thought.

That's when he finally started paying me right and treating me like a true partner. It took a whole fucking *year* and support from his own crew for that to happen. But once I started making my own deals and running my own shit, he could finally *see* that I knew what I was doing. And I was better than him at it to boot. I actually *paid* people what they were worth and treated them better, which made them want to work for me and look out for me. But still, I remained loyal to Cisco and took him back up on his offer to make bigger money together, so I made another run for him.

The problem was, Cisco didn't make twenty-eight-thousand dollars like he *said* we would. Instead, he came up with more excuses not to pay me what he said he would. He was the most dishonest businessman I had ever known. I couldn't trust anything he said anymore. But since I was right there in the middle of it with him, I kept trying to make our personal and business relationship work. It was a lot easier to do that with someone you were still sleeping with. I guess my emotions continued to cloud my business mind and get the best of me. However, our money issues from the dope game was starting to create a lot more tension between us, especially once I learned how to make my own in it.

Then I found out that Cisco had a *wife* in Atlanta! A dancer I knew from the Atlanta area told me that she saw him up there at a funeral with a woman and two daughters.

I told myself, *No wonder he never has any money; she probably gets it all in Atlanta.*

I was shocked and confused by the whole thing.

How could this nigga spend so much time with *me*, while he still had a *wife* in another state? What kind of marriage was that anyway? Was he telling her that he was doing business down in Miami? So I became skeptical about *everything*!

When I confronted Cisco about it, he never tried to deny it. He told me point blank, "That's my wife and daughters, but we're getting a divorce. We've been separated for *years* now. We just haven't done it yet."

"Well, when do you *plan* to?" I asked him. I felt like my fucking *mother* when she found out about Jose years ago. My mother was still sick and living a mental home in Atlanta over that shit. Now it was *my* turn.

"Soon," Cisco told me. "So don't worry about her. All this time I've been with *you*."

Yeah, but did he *respect* me. I don't believe he ever *did*, and I had been running around for a damn *year*, fucking and delivering drugs for a married-ass man! And I *still* didn't leave him after I found out about it. Talk about being *loyal*. I was *crazy* in love, like Beyonce and Jay.

By the time I found out, I was twenty-three years old and had been dating him nearly a year. I was already deep in love with the man and tied to his business. But once I found out that he was married, I would always get angry and use it against him.

"Why don't you just go back to your *wife* in Atlanta and leave me alone," I told him. But I was confused and never really meant it. It was the same pitiful shit I had gone through with Travis when he told me he had gotten another girl pregnant. But a pregnancy was the last thing I wanted in my life. Having kids would have tied me down to that man *for real*. So I had been on birth control since my teenage years to avoid kids. I wasn't having it.

Yet and still, each time Cisco would do me wrong, I would listen to his begging, lying and pleading and let him back into my heart and bed again, while always trying to make new money with him. I should have never gotten involved and then *stayed* involved with a cheap, married, dope-dealing, disrespect and *abusive* older man to begin with. But that's an unloved young woman for you. I didn't know which way was up, and I had never been around a perfect household situation to know how to find or create one of my own. Cisco was *who* and *what* I had settled down with at the time. In the twisted game of life, if you deal with the wrong people, you can sometimes turn you into a lovesick fool.

But through it all, I kept my eyes on the prize of running Dior's World Entertainment promotions company by myself one day and not dealing with anything else from anyone, including Cisco.

2nd Year of Cisco

Even though I *knew* my relationship with Cisco had nowhere good to go, I continued to try and work it out with him for a second year. I was still in love, we were making good money together, my living expenses were all taken care of and I still felt comfortable. Then we moved from our townhouse in North Miami into a new condo in Aventura.

When we moved into this new place, we made it look incredible, with all new furniture, artwork, paintings, a Jacuzzi bath—*everything*. Then Cisco started inviting his company over to the house to show the place off, and I didn't like that. Whether it was for business or personal, I didn't want people being up in my space like that. Remember, I had been living on my own since graduating from high school and I wasn't used to having a bunch of company over unless it was my family. I didn't even like my family being in my space to be honest. That's why I put my sister Naomi up in her own place. So Cisco and I started to argue about that too.

He said, "All right, I'ma go get another little place for me then."

"Fine. Do what you gotta do," I told him. "But don't bring that stuff over *here*. I don't want all of those people up in my face like that."

You know, I would come home some nights ready to relax and kick back, and he would have all these guys hanging out everywhere. I didn't feel like entertaining or hosting any of them. They weren't *my* company and I wasn't really social like that to begin with. I wasn't the happy, trophy housewife type, and we weren't even *married.* So I put a stop to that shit *immediately.* I just didn't support him trying to turn me into some kind of *showpiece* for his friends with the rest of the artwork and furniture.

Cisco didn't really support me in my promotion business either. Sure, he would continue to put up half the money and take half of the split, but that was it. It wasn't as if he really *cared* about how well I was doing with it or showed any interest in what I was doing. I had become so successful at promotions that I stopped stripping at clubs all together. But Cisco didn't care.

I started charging twenty-five dollars for tickets in advance and forty at the door, making up to fifty-thousand dollars on some nights. Then I started booking more celebrity guests for good deals, like the rapper Scarface, who came through for only six thousand and allowed us to make another fifteen.

I even started up a promotions night at The Uno with Don as the new owner. The Uno still needed to some new energy, ideas and business on the slow nights, especially since Big Pete was no longer running it. But then Don started worrying about me competing with The Uno by having other promotions nights at Primadonna's.

He told me, "Dior, why you gotta do things with them. I thought you had some *loyalty* to The Uno. Didn't we help to get you started?"

I said, "I am loyal to The Uno, that's why I'm still doing business with you. There's enough out here for both of us. I mean, I promote there on different nights. But I throw parties now, that's what I do."

It wasn't like I could make money at The Uno every night. So Don backed down and let me do my thing. I established Porno Star Wednesdays at Primadonna's, where I continued to invite special guests from the porn movie industry, and then started Double Up Thursdays at

The Uno, where you could get two shots of drinks for the price of one. I was moving forward with my plans to become my own businesswoman, whether Cisco realized it or not.

But just like with Trini in St. Thomas, Cisco didn't want me dancing anymore. At this one promotions event, he overheard one of my old customers saying, "Damn, Dior still looking *good* up in here. I wouldn't mind fucking the shit out of her."

Cisco didn't like hearing that at all, and he told me about it.

He said, "Yo, you don't need to dance and shit anymore, you're already getting good money. That shit is beneath you now. Let the other bitches do that."

Even though he said it out of jealousy, that shit stuck with me. I had always wanted to stop dancing, but I kept making excuses for myself to get back in it. But Cisco was right. I finally was making money without dancing. So I forced myself not to do it. And if I needed more money, I would just hustle my parties harder.

Cisco still wanted me to be up under him. But once I saw how I could make my own money on the regularly—*legally*—from my club promotions, I wasn't really feeling the dope game anymore. It was just a quick means to an end and definitely not a lifestyle for me, but Cisco didn't see it that way.

Then I messed around and got *pregnant* in that second year of living with him. I was twenty-four year old by then and had never been pregnant before. I had been taking birth control ever since I moved out on my own as a teenager, but after I saw my OBGYN in my twenties, he continued to tell me that my body needed a *rest* from it. It had been on birth control five, six, seven years *straight*, and I was told that if I ever wanted to have kids and a normal cycle one day, that I needed to allow my body to go through a natural process again.

It took me a minute to listen, but then I finally decided to stop taking my pills and allow my body a chance to rest. Now, up until then, I had still been protecting myself with the use of condoms and everything, but I wouldn't trip out if I slipped up or if a condom broke. Then Cisco and I slipped up this one time without a condom after I had stopped using my birth control, and I fucking got pregnant.

I couldn't *believe* it! After all of that time of taking birth control to avoid pregnancies, I really didn't believe that my body could conceive that fast, but it did.

I saw my doctor for another check up and he was like, "Yes, you are. You're almost *two months.*"

I was like, "What?"

They did a urine test and then showed me the sonogram picture on a computer monitor, while letting me hear the baby's heartbeat in the fetus stage.

Oh my *God!* I was scared to death and didn't know what to do about it. I was *shocked,* man. The experience was all new to me. So I started calling up family members before I said anything to Cisco about it.

My Cisco Naomi was excited about it. "Oh, girl, that's *great.* Is it a boy or a girl?"

She was going all into detail about it.

I said, "I don't know, Naomi. I didn't ask them all of that."

I was still trying to decide whether I wanted to keep it or not. But Naomi was adamant because she was already a mother.

She was like, "Keep it, Keisha, *keep it.*"

My middle sister Charmaine had a baby by that time too, but I still didn't talk to her much. During that time I went into an emotional shell and didn't want to really talk to anyone. Then I started reaching out my mother on the regular t talk to her about it.

My mother was still sick and staying in a mental

181

hospital in Atlanta at the time, but I still valued her advice and opinions. So she started telling me more health related things for if I decided to keep the baby, you know about the rights foods to eat, exercise, vitamins and proteins and all of that stuff. But I still hadn't made up my mind yet. I kept thinking about how it would change my life and tie me down to Cisco, and I didn't know if I was ready for that. I still looked forward to the reality of moving on from him soon.

So when I finally got around to telling him that I was pregnant, Cisco flipped out.

"You're pregnant? You can't be pregnant. I thought you were on birth control."

I knew how that conversation was going to sound before I even said anything. It was going to look like I had set him up to have a baby, but I really didn't. I wasn't even *thinking* about having a baby with Cisco. I was thinking all about love and money, but the *love* was actually getting in the way, because Cisco still owed me *thousands* of dollars and he was still not helping me enough in my promotions business as much as he could have been.

Anyway, I told him, "The doctors told me to stop using it to give my body a rest."

"Well, how come you didn't tell me that?"

"I didn't get around to it yet."

That sounded lame, but it was the truth. We were still using protection most of the time, so what did it even matter?

Cisco said, "Well, I can't have no baby with you. I already have a wife and two daughters and that's *enough* for me right now. I got too much going on for another baby right now."

As usual, it was all about *him*. He didn't consider *my* feelings in the matter at all. I didn't want to have a baby *either*, but it happened. I also didn't believe in abortions, so when Cisco started pressuring me to have one, I pretty much tried to stay away from him. We weren't even talking to each other at that time, while still living in the same house. Then he stopped coming back, like he didn't want to even deal with me anymore.

I was so pressed about my decision that I thought about talking to my father and brothers for a masculine perspective. I was just trying to understand how a man would look at it, because I knew my sister Naomi was too damned excited for me to keep it. But then I decided to go ahead and have an abortion, because having a baby with a drug-dealing man, who already had a wife and kids and who didn't really want to be with me like that would have been *stupid*. I was still being used by Cisco, and the way he flaked out on me while pregnant made it obvious.

So I called him up a few weeks before the third trimester and said, "All right, let's go have this abortion and just get it over with it." I knew that I couldn't drive myself back home after the procedure, and Cisco was ready to pay for it. So I let him do it.

I figured it was the best thing to do because I knew that I would never be happy in that situation. But it wasn't *easy*. You see your baby's picture on a sonogram screen and hear its heartbeat and you can never get that out of your mind. I even kept the picture that they gave from the printout to remind myself of what I had done.

I told my father about it after it was done, and at first he was speechless. Then he said, "I don't know what to say. But no matter what, you know that I'll *always* here to support you."

I knew that my father wouldn't have that much to say about it. That's just how he was. He was more supportive by what he *did*, not by what he *said*. He was old school that way. But I just wanted him to *know* about it. I felt like I needed to tell my family so that I could *heal* from it. I even wrote my brother Contrell a letter about it in prison to see what he would say. Pat Pat wrote me back

183

and said that I had made the right decision.

He was like, "You don't need to be having no baby with a married nigga no way. So you made the right choice."

He was very *firm* about it. And Naomi had to get over it, because I wasn't going down that road to allow myself to choose to live with more hardships and arguing. And from that moment on, I knew that my relationship with Cisco was finally over. He tried to act like everything would go back to normal and that I would still want to be all up under him like old times, but that wasn't happening.

When I went under the knife for that abortion, it was like my ties to Cisco had died as well, and I was no longer willing to put up with his shit. I didn't even want him to touch me *sexually* anymore. We barely spoke or looked each other in the face. I just didn't want to have anything to do with him. And the next thing I knew, he stopped coming around the house. Then I heard that he was spending more time in Atlanta, trying working things out with his wife, so he surely wouldn't missing me.

Well, since he name wasn't on the lease anyway—with everything in my name—I took his ass off the guest list too and started paying my own mortgage. Then I changed my phone numbers, like good riddance. And once I had finally told myself that it was over, there was nothing I could do to change my emotions. I had gone through a lot with that man and the abortion was the final straw for my mind, body and soul to sever the ties with him for good. And that's what I did. There was no conversation needed. I moved right on to focusing on me and my promotions business—*finally*. It was all about Dior's World Entertainment.

Time For My Own Shit

Once I moved on from my relationship with Cisco and closed that chapter of my life's book, I had no one else to depend on but myself. I was leaving behind access to exotic cars, trucks, money and lavish luxury with Cisco, and I knew that he may try to destroy me out of jealousy and envy, but I was *done* with him, and knew that I needed to get on with my life. It was just time for me to build my own shit, and I couldn't trust my future in anyone else's hands anymore.

By that time, I knew everything there was to know about the strip clubs, the streets *and* the dope game like a pro. I had watched all of the guys and women in my circle for *years*, so it was time for me step up and work with what I knew on my own. But after leaving Cisco, I only had five-thousand dollars to my name. Usually, I had access to a lot more money, but again, I had to learn how to work with what I had.

At first I panicked and started thinking about going back to stripping. I can't even lie. I knew that I could make money with stripping. But then I asked myself, *Why would you do that? Just keep making dope money.*

I figured I could keep my own dope game and make it bigger and better than Cisco had his with more loyalty and better money decisions. The only problem was, without Cisco around to co-sign the deals that I made, I would have start back over from scratch. And I didn't really like that idea. What it somebody tried to play me for my money? Then I would have to pay an enforcer to get it back with nothing to pay them with. And I only had five-thousand dollars to work with. So ultimately, I didn't feel secure enough to get back into the dope game without more money on me. That made me jump back into the club promotions business, which was something I could afford.

Even though the club promoters knew that Cisco had been my partner, they were more concerned about business than old loyalty. They just wanted to make sure that I could still do a success, money-making event by myself. But it wasn't as if Cisco had done any of the real promotions *work* anyway. All he had ever done was help me to finance it. I was the one with all of the celebrity contacts, who was reaching out to people and setting up the deals. So my transition was only about having the upfront money to keep my promotions going.

The short white man named Don, who was running The Uno at the time, wanted me back badly to keep promoting parties there. Basically, he didn't know what he was doing, and he knew that I did. But I found out that Cisco had been going out of his way to badmouth me to the club owners and other promoters. So when I went to set up my meetings to push my own business without him, some of these guys told me about it.

"You partner Cisco told me not to deal with you. He said you had a bad attitude and was not good in business."

I heard that same thing from a couple of people I knew, so I knew it was true. That's just how Cisco was. But sometimes I couldn't *believe* how vindictive he was. So I had to keep telling people that he was no longer my partner.

I was like, "Shit, dude, move on with your fucking *life*!" Why was he still trying so hard to throw a bucket of water on my shit? But fuck him. I had to keep it *hot* and keep it *moving*. And that's what I did.

Then I found out *why* Cisco was trying so hard to bring my promotions business down. He was still trying to promote parties too. He contacting the club owners and promoters, and trying to run his own ideas through them. He even set up a party with a promoter I knew named Travis SW. Travis was pretty big in Miami too.

Cisco set up this event with Travis where they were supposed to have this Atlanta rapper named Young Scooter come down to perform his song called *Columbia* or whatever. But he never even showed up. It was embarrassing. Shit like that never happened at my parties. The people I invited would show up and have a good time because I made sure I had a good relationship when them first. But Cisco wasn't like that. He never really nurtured personal relationships. So when Travis came to me about it, he already knew that Cisco was about some bullshit.

He said, "I tried to do something with your boy Cisco, but it didn't work out." Then he said he wanted to do some parties with me. After dealing with Cisco, Travis realized that I was the real brains behind Dior's World Entertainment and he knew that I had the real contacts to the special guests that I would reach out to.

He was like, "Dior, me and you should do some parties together. Call me and let's talk about it to figure something out."

I said, "All right, I'll do that. I'll think about it."

At first, I was just being cordial about the business, because I really wanted to start doing my own thing without partners. But once I thought about it, I decided that Travis SW had a big name of his own in promotions, and sharing the expenses and the marketing with him would be a good idea. So I called him back up and we did some combined promotions as Travis SW and Dior's World Entertainment.

I'm sure Cisco didn't like when he heard about that either, but he would have to deal with the fact that I was a better business partner than he was.

So I set up my meetings with the club owners to get back in the promotions game, and I plenty of people who were still willing to join forces with me. I was back on my own, but I was still smart enough to know that partnerships cut the risk of doing business, and I was used to having a partner to share the risks with. But I still set everything up with my contacts. I just wanted to make that everything was right. I didn't want any guests not showing up at my parties.

I remember at the end of 2012, Travis and I set up a party called the Sagittarian Bash of the Year, hosted by Grammy-winning music producer Rico Love and the rapper Trina. We had it at The Uno and the place was packed out to the wall. The capacity was usually around a hundred-seventy-five or whatever, but he had it packed at two hundred to two-*fifty* that night. No one was complaining about it though. They all had a *ball*.

Honestly, I didn't expect the standing-room-only crowd like that. I was still kind of nervous about this new partnership and wondering if things would all work out. But once it did, it gave me the confidence to know that I was *back*. And I started getting big money again. Travis and I split eight-thousand dollars from The Uno party that night. That allowed me to get back into the dope game with money to buy new packages and hook back up with my old team from Boston. I still wasn't willing to give up that fast street money yet, and I didn't think the club promotions was enough for me.

So I got back to picking up packages and dropping it off to Boston and his crew to cut it and make money with me. I didn't really touch the stuff outside of picking it up and dropping it off. My hands were not in that part. I would collect anywhere from twelve to twenty-thousand dollars from a package. So the money was good.

I had basically duplicated the hustle that I learned

from Cisco and I didn't want to stop it. I was used to having multiple hustles.

After awhile, I even broke out and got my own place in downtown Miami. As they say, fast money spends fast. So I left Cisco's place with twelve-hundred dollars a month for rent, to my own downtown condo, paying twenty-three-hundred dollars a month. Then I had to buy all new furniture. I bought a bunch of white leather, silver metallic lamps and lights and a mustard-colored carpet with lots of mirrors on the walls. It was all lavish and tasteful, and most importantly it was all *mine.*

I didn't take any of Cisco's furniture with me. So the Colombia owner of the condo building had it all taken out, including Cisco's leftover clothes and things that never picked up. The bad part about it was that *I* had to pay for all that shit to be moved, because Cisco wasn't on the lease and was no longer there.

I said, "All right. Whatever." So I paid what I had to pay and moved on from it.

I was making good money in the dope game to keep paying my expensive habits, but the strip club promotions was really my first love. I thought more about promoting parties than anything, and it made me feel the best and the most accomplished. I felt greedy and paranoid most the time in the dope game. You always had to be thinking about watching your back. But in the promotions game, I was able to have a good time and deal with celebrities on a regular basis without the extra drama of getting my money or product taken, being arrested or shot out over stupid turf war bullshit.

Fortunately, I didn't have any of that happen to me. My dope game was hustled had been smooth with no hassles, mainly because Boston and his crew knew that they could trust me to be fair t them. We all like *family* after dealing with Cisco. And no one wanted to go back to him, so they dealt with me.

This one time though, when I went to pick up a package, the ghetto-ass neighborhood that I was in had another Toyota Corolla that the police were looking for, and the police jumped out on me when I stopped at the corner.

They were like, "Police! This is a raid! Get out of the car!"

They had guns drawn and everything. I was like, "*Shit!*" because the jump out police had come out nowhere. Then I kept my cool while they searched through the car. I had a special compartment behind the stereo system that I used to hide the dope packages I bought, and without any police dogs there to sniff it out, they didn't find anything.

But let me tell you, while the police searched my car that day, my ass was standing there sweating *bricks* again. I was nervous as hell, but I *refused* to let them see me panic. I would have looked guilty if I did that. So once they didn't find anything, I asked them, "God, is everything all right?"

I didn't want to act *too* cool about it. I mean, anybody would be concerned about a bunch of cops jumping out on you in the middle of the street. And it was embarrassing with people watching me.

Then the cops got all apologetic. "Oh, we're sorry, we're sorry. We were looking for a Toyota like yours."

I didn't even ask them what they were looking for in it. It was none of my business. I just wanted to get out of there. I kept telling myself, *Why are you even doing this shit anymore?* It was fast money, but I didn't need to do it and my promotions game was taking off again. And that became the last dope package I ever bought or dealt with. I didn't tell Boston and my team though. I just kind of blew it off.

I said, "You know what? I got some other things I want to do know with my party promotions or whatever. So I'm gonna take a little break for a minute."

I didn't have to be all up in their face about it. They knew that I was already involved in the party promotions game and respected me that way. So they left it alone. Boston and his crew were doing their business by that time anyway. And whenever they called me up to check back in with me, I always told them that I was good. I didn't need to get back into the street game.

By the spring of 2013, I was twenty-five years old I had decided to dedicate myself to my promotions company—Dior's World Entertainment—with nothing else. I just figured I would have to force myself to bite the bullet and learn how to budget what I made to pay off everything and keep it going. I was an adult, who had been living on my own since my teenage years, so I needed to relearn how to budget my. I had been doing it for *years* before shacking up with Cisco, so I had to relearn how to do it.

I started traveling to different cities like New York, Boston, Atlanta and the Caribbean Islands, attending concerts, parties and even big fight events out in Las Vegas. I was finally having a good time and enjoying my life, while still making connections and studying the promotions hustle in other places. I wanted to keep learning and continue to build confidence with new ideas about what I was doing.

If you don't already know it, then you have to do what you have to do to learn it. So that's what I was doing. I was making my own personal connections with the right people up and down the East Coast, out in the country and down in the islands. I found that that's where the money really was—networking.

Miami was still my home, but it was only one city, and there was money to get *everywhere*. You feel me? So I was out to get with no more fear about the unknown. I had been through a lot in young my life already and nothing really scared me. I was just fucking going for it,

191

making money promoting parties and living my life.

I also continued to look like money to get folks attention when I needed to. Shit, I *liked* to dress like money. You have to look like what you wanted. If you want big money you have to look like big money. If want big things to happen, then you have *make* big things happen. Things are not going to come to you without calling for it. So I played my part to attract people to me.

I wore Versace, Chanel and Gucci dresses. I had my Louis Vuitton and Chanel bags. I had Burberry and Gucci belts and different designer perfumes. And don't get me started naming all the shoes and boots that continued to buy and wear. Everywhere I went to let the people know that Dior was up in the damn building. But the one thing I didn't have was access Cisco's cars anymore. I used to drive a Mercedes S500, a Bentley and a Range Rover. Nevertheless, I had my new freedom and peace of mind to do my own business and live my own life without needing to depend on anyone. And I considered that *priceless*.

Along with traveling and networking, I started using social media to help promote my events and reach out to more people on Twitter, Facebook and Instagram, including a bunch of other celebrities and people online. I met Meek Mills from Philly, the singer K. Michelle, DMX and Rick Ross online. Some of the people I met on social media would even stop by at my events when they were in town in Miami.

Then I started following *New York Times* best-selling author Omar Tyree on Twitter and reached out to him. I had read his book *Flyy Girl* years ago in my teenage years, and I had always admired his ability to tell a story, particularly from a *girl's* point of view. I thought it was unique for a guy to be able to do that and to understand a young woman well enough write a best-selling book about her. Omar had done that with several of books from a girl's perspective.

I had read his book *Leslie* about this crazy Haitian and Black Indian girl from New Orleans. *Diary of a Groupie* about this orphan from Las Vegas, who sleeps with a lot of celebrities. I read *For The Love of Money* and *Boss Lady*, the two sequels to *Flyy Girl*. I even read some of his guy books, like *Just Say No!* about this R&B singer addicted drugs, women and *everything*. He was a real *mess*.

So I got this idea to ask Omar to help me write *my* book. I thought I had been through enough in my life with the strip club and my family for a good read. And who would know better about putting it together than Omar Tyree?

I had never been shy, scared or bashful about reaching out to people. Everyone was *human* to me, no matter *who* they were, and they all wanted to make money. So I tweeted to Omar one day that we could make some good money writing about my life in the strip clubs. With all of the people that strip clubs touched, who came in to spend money with us, I just *knew* that it was a good subject to write a about. There was no doubt in my mind. In my opinion, a book about the strip club life was a *goldmine*!

To my surprise, Omar responded back to me immediately, but he was talking more about a consultation and writing service to explain to me how to write my own book.

I was like, "*Shit*, he responded." I was halfway there. But then I said, "I don't know shit about writing books." I thought it would be extremely time consuming, and I was always on the go. So I knew that I needed to talk Omar into helping me to write it, even if I had to pay him for it. So I hit him up again and gave him my cell number, telling him to contact me to talk about it.

Business is business, you know. And like clockwork, he hit me back and asked me when would be the best time to call. I was like, "Anytime!" and was mad excited. I *knew* that I would talk him into helping me. I even started telling my family about it.

"Oh my *God*, Naomi, Omar Tyree hit me back on Twitter! I want to try and talk him into helping me to write my own book."

Naomi said, "For real? You think he'll do it?"

"I'm gonna *see*. So far, so good," I told her.

Then I called my father and told him about it.

He said, "That's good. That online network stuff really works, huh?"

Technology had made a lot of things easier. I said, "Yeah, I use social media *a lot* now. That's the new *world* we live in."

Then my father asked me, "So, what would the book be about?"

"About my life in the strip clubs," I answered. "I've been through a lot out here the past few years, and so have a lot of other girls who dance in the clubs. But I don't really see a lot of books about that. So I would have him to write all about my life."

My father said, "Yeah, that sounds like a good idea. Go for it."

I was thrilled that my father was still so supportive with everything I did. That gave me a lot of confidence. So I was ready to run down my book ideas to Omar as soon as he called me.

I remember the first time he called; I was shocked by how deep his voice was. He was like, "Hey, this is Omar Tyree," sounding cooler than I thought he would.

I can't even lie, I thought he would sound *nerdy*, you know, like a company executive or something. I hadn't met or talked to a writer of his stature before. But he sounded like a regular guy from the 'hood, so I started telling him how much I admired his work with *Flyy Girl*.

He said, "Yeah, everybody likes that book. I guess I got lucky with that one. I just wish they would read some of my other books."

Omar had written like twenty-something books and he said that people talked about *Flyy Girl* as if it was the only book he had written. Like I had mentioned, I had read a lot of his books, *Flyy Girl* just struck a chord with a lot of young girls in the 'hood. There were many urban girls growing up in hard times, trying to make money and good decisions I life just like "Tracy" in the book, so I think we all *related* to it. But I knew what Omar was saying. If guys only talked about one outfit that I wore in the strip clubs, or only one pair of boots, I would want to talk about my other outfits and boots too. But you always have your *favorites*. After being around plenty of Haitians, growing in Miami—including Cisco—I liked Omar's book *Leslie* a lot too. That girl was *crazy*. She totally freaked me out!

Anyway, with books on my mind, I got right down to business and told him that I wanted to write one about my life in the strip clubs. I started rambling on about everything I had been through to let him know that the book would be *filled* with drama, and he listened to it all calmly.

Then he said, "Yeah, I have a consultation service, where I could show you everything you need to know and put you in touch with all the right people to help you to make it happen."

I was thinking, *For what? I got you on the phone right now. How come you can't help me to make it happen?*

I listened to his whole speech about hiss consultation service, knowing full well that I had to talk him into helping me to write it, because he wasn't seeing it that way. It was like he holding up a brick wall to my suggestions, and he only wanted to show me *how*.

I thought, *Okay, what do I need to do? Do I need to offer him some the money, fly out to see him for some good head and pussy, or what?*

I didn't want to do my business like that, but hell, I

thought about it. I just felt like I was so *close*, having conversations about books with the man who wrote *Flyy Girl*, and I just needed to get him onboard by any means necessary.

Once I had Omar's number to discuss his consultation service, I figured I would map it all out and keep pushing for what I *really* wanted—for *Omar* to write it. So I agreed to do the consultation just to stay in business with him. He was only asking for two-hundred-fifty dollars to sign up for it, and I could make that much in my *sleep*. So I signed up and paid him immediately. But the next time I spoke to him on the phone, I went for the jugular.

Omar was explaining to me how to pull a book together with his ten-step program or whatever, but I like, "You know what? I really don't know how to write a book. And I move around too much for that. I'm still promoting my parties and traveling a lot. So how much would I have to pay you to write it for me?"

He stopped explaining shit and said, "Umm… if you want me to ghostwrite, that would cost you a lot more money." But he never said how much.

Then he said that he had just finished working on a book for Marion Barry, the old mayor of Washington, DC, who was caught up in a hotel room smoking crack with a woman.

"Let me think about that," he told me.

Man, I was ready to *force* the issue. I just felt like Omar would be *perfect* to write my book. So I told him, "How 'bout I fly up there this weekend and treat you to a basketball game on something and we talk about it after."

Looking at all of his tweets, I could tell that Omar was really into sports, and I liked basketball too. It didn't seem like the head and pussy game would work for him anyway. He was too much into his business, and I knew the type—money over everything. So I wanted to offer him something else to try and close the deal with.

He said, "For real? You would do that?" He sounded shocked by my urgent offer, but I was dead *serious* about getting him to write my book.

I said, "Yeah, the Lakers are playing. That's a good game with Kobe."

Kobe Bryant was just coming back from his injury.

Omar said, "Well, I got an event in South Carolina this weekend, but I should be able to make it back for the game."

Perfect! That was all I needed to hear. I had frequent flyer miles and everything, so I booked a cheap flight and kept texting him back to make sure he could make it to the game on time before I paid for two tickets.

He called me back before I ordered the seats and said, "It's raining pretty bad down here and this book club wants to treat me to dinner, so I won't be able to rush back in the rain in time for the game. You go ahead and enjoy it yourself, and I'll catch up to you afterwards."

I was like, "Cool." And that's what I did. I bought a ticket with a seat right up close to the Lakers team bench and enjoyed the game. But then it got so late that Omar said he couldn't meet me at all that night. He said he would have to meet me in the morning instead.

Man, I was *pissed.* You fly out to meet a nigga and talk business with him, and you wait a whole day and night to do it without seeing him, while he's telling you some, "I'll see you in the morning" shit?

I told myself, "If this motherfucker wasted my damn time and money..." I was ready to through his damn books away and badmouth him if he didn't show up. It didn't rain all fucking night. So that was some *bullshit.* So I felt like he was blowing me off and didn't take me seriously.

But that next morning, Omar Tyree met me at my hotel bright and early for breakfast like he said he would, well before my return flight to Miami.

He was taller than I thought he would be in real life too, and younger looking. He almost looked like a *kid* in man's body, but he was dressed for business with a sports jacket, dress shirt and shoes.

He said, "I'm sorry I couldn't meet up with you last night, but you put a lot on mind to think about with how you were pressing me. So I had to sit down and go over everything. And I didn't know how serious you were."

I said, "Oh no, I'm *very* serious." Of course, Omar didn't know me yet, but I was *always* pressed for business. With five and six years in the strip club life, hustling and being around money twenty-four-seven, I had *definitely* learned how to be a *hustler* and I wouldn't take *no* for answer.

He smiled and said, "Yeah, I get a lot of people who bullshit and think that writing books is cheap and easy, but it's *not*. It's a lot of *time* and *experience* that goes into this. This is my *profession*, not some *hobby*."

I nodded and said, "I know. You don't get to be a *New York Times* best-seller by bullshitting. That's why I wanted to fly up her to meet you, face to face."

He said, "Yeah, that impressed me. I wasn't ready for that. That's some movie-type shit, not regular broke people."

I laughed it off and said, "Oh, I'm *never* broke. In the strip club business, there's thousands of dollars around you every day. And I do mean, *every* day."

Omar ordered scrambled eggs, bacon, pancakes and orange juice before he ran down a bunch of ideas that he had thought about before meeting me. He started talking about writing a strip club stage play, doing a strip club tour, marketing nationwide and a whole bunch of other stuff. But I just wanted him to write my damn *book*. I wasn't prepared for everything else that he was talking about. I guess his hustle ideas were bigger than *mine*. So I listened to him and all, but I paid more attention when he came back to the part about the books.

"Okay, so you told me you have other girls who want to tell their stories too, right?" he asked me.

I was like, "Yeah, a know *lots* of girls with a story to tell. I can line them up for you right now, but I want to pick only the *best*."

"Well, what you need to do is create a book *series* then," he told me. "That lets the readers know that you have more of the same to come. That's how folks like to read books now; everything is about the *series*. And your book would be the *first*."

As a strip club promoter, who had gotten comfortable with the business of paying strippers for their services, I started thinking about paying for their stories under my wing too, so I liked the idea.

Omar said, "So we need to brand a *title* that will allow you to do that."

He kept talking about using *The Strip Club Diaries* as the title, like *The Vampire Diaries*. But I wanted to use something more like, *The Confessions of a Stripper*.

Omar said, "Yeah, but that's only *one* book. You don't want to use a title like that if you're trying to build a *series*. And that whole *'confessions'* word is worn out to me."

He sounded like a man with strong opinions about the book industry. But the main thing was that he was agreeing to write it with me. So we discussed the price and went back and forth with it until we both agreed on a number that we could accept. Then I had to make my flight back home to Miami, while feeling *great* that morning. It was mission accomplished, and I couldn't *wait* to tell everybody. But I had to get my money up to do it. So I started shifting my gears and pulling all of my money together from spending it in ten different ways to prepare for this big mission of writing my book.

Then it took us *weeks* to come up with the final title,

or at least it did for me. Omar was adamant about using *The Strip Club Diaries* because it was the most obvious for readers to remember. But other people I asked wanted something different from the obvious. So we thought about using exotic dancers, pole artists, adult entertainers, midnight vixens and a few other words outside of using *strippers*, but Omar wouldn't budge.

He said, "Keisha, at the end of the day, you can use all of these fancy words if you want, but we're still talking about *strippers* and the *strip club*. That's what we really *call it*. So to go away from that only makes it harder for you to brand and market the books. You want to name it something that people are familiar with and will call out immediately. 'Oh yeah, *The Strip Club Diaries*.' Then I would just use your club name, Dior as number one. We do *The Strip Club Diaries* number two with Candy, *The Strip Club Diaries* number three with Marsha, and you keep it going like that."

He said, "All you need to do is change the names and image on the cover of each individual book and story."

I was still unsure about it myself, but Omar's idea made a lot of sense. If you number the books like; one, two, three and four, the readers would naturally buy them as a *group*, as long as they liked them, and mine would come *first*. Then he asked me for pictures to design the cover jacket with, which was another process.

Omar showed me the first design ideas from his cover artist, and let me know how he would improve it. And by the time the cover was ready to go—with my picture on it and my name Dior in neon lights—the final design looked *incredible*.

I was like, "Damn, that's *hot*!"

Omar said, "All you have to do now is change the name, the colors and the girl for each new book, and keep the same design so folks can recognize it, and you're *good*, over and over and over again. That's how you brand a book series or *anything*. Everything has to be in sync and easy to duplicate."

From there, we set up an outline for the book to see how much we would cover, and I bought a recorder device and started taping my life. Omar would follow up with a bunch of questions to add clarity and details, and we started the long, three-month process of putting my book together, which was tedious as hell, especially since I didn't want to use everyone's real names or put their personal business out there.

Omar advised me, "You can just say that it's *based* off your life. That way, you don't have to say everything and you can change whatever you want to make a point. That's why I write *fiction*. It gives you a chance to bend the story the way you need to, but it's still based on the *facts*. Everything you say about the strip club life would be *real*, and that's what people care about it; just be on point with your *facts*."

I had plenty of facts to talk about. But as we began to work on my book, Omar wanted to add a bunch of things that really didn't happen to me. I had learned to *control* a lot of the shit that I got involved in, but I couldn't say that about some of the other girls.

I said, "Don't worry, when we get to books two and three, these other girls got some *shit* you're your *ass*. I can't *believe* some of them things that these girls went through or were involved in."

So I looked at my book as the introduction to the series with me as the Queen Bee. I was much more on the money side in my world than the drama. But every girl didn't end up in control of their lives like I did. The main thing I was concerned about was representing my family right. My mother didn't even know that I was into strip clubs until years after I had started. But I couldn't hide it from her forever. And at first, she tripped out about it.

I saw my mother up in Atlanta one time, while she was still sick, and she told me, "How *dare* you do something like that? I didn't raise you that way. And how did you let your sister do it?"

I can't even remember how my mother found out about it. I know I never told her. But once she knew, I said, "Mom, but you were away from us for like, five years. What was I supposed to do? I have to care for Naomi, and my regular job wasn't making enough money. It wasn't as if I *wanted* to be a stripper."

My mother started talking about education and going back to school, but you have to pay for that too. I mean, at least I *tried* to do it. But it's *hard* when you need money to pay for *everything*, including your younger siblings. Most college students have their *parents* to help pay for that shit. So my mother calmed down and got over it. It wasn't if I was emotionally scared *for life* or anything. I had found how to move on from stripping.

Eventually, my mother moved back to Miami, where she started to spend time between me and my two sisters; Naomi and Charmaine. My mother was still in and out of her spells of anxiety about what she had gone through with Jose, but at least she wasn't spazing out and leaving us anymore. And she still had her own money from long ago property deals that she had made. I guess I got some of my hustle from my mother.

My sister Naomi matured and got involved in better things too. She stopped stripping years before I did and went back to school for a nursing program to become a registered nurse. She had another child—a daughter—with her new Haitian boyfriend and was raising her family like regular adult. And I was *proud* of her.

I still can't say I made mends with my sister Charmaine though. Real life isn't some big fairytale. So I can't tell you what Charmaine has been up to. She's pretty much raising her daughter as a single mom with her own place, but we still don't really talk like that. Maybe we will one day, but as for now... we just *don't*. I can't even explain. We just live our separate lives like distance cousins or something. We just never had that strong sister connection.

I haven't been around my brothers much either. After Henry and Myshion both moved to Missouri for the construction business, Myshion ended up having a baby from two different women, and Henry dropped the girlfriend he moved out there for and two kids with another woman. Then he relocated to Alabama and had two more kids with another woman. So I have nieces and nephews all over the place now. It takes a minute for me to try and even name them all.

Then my oldest brother Pat Pat got out of jail in early 2013—in the middle of my focus on my promotions business—and he fell right back into the street game with dope and went straight back to jail. I don't even think he was out on the street for a half a *year* before he got arrested again. It's like that old song; *street life is the only life I know.*

My brother Contrell was still set in his own ways, and nobody could tell him anything. He didn't even try to let any of us help him before he did that shit. So now he's having more court cases to figure out what's going to happen next, which had been the story of my oldest brother's life.

Really, talking about my family was the hardest part of this book. How can any girl be honest about the people she loves and grew up with when times were hard—especially in the life of a stripper? It's not like that's the best career for a girl to have, but it's *real*, and we're real-ass people. So when my father read some of the earlier chapters from my book, where I talked about the big fight he had with my mother when we were kids, he didn't like that shit. I guess he didn't want to remember it or have people to read about it, but it's my life, and we all had to move on from it. Even Naomi had to learn how to talk to my father again.

But I can't write a book about my life and try to act like that shit never happened. How would that look? Your early family life it what shapes what you do later on. Everybody knows that. But that doesn't mean that I don't *love* my father. If you look at how many times I ask him for his opinions and came to him to tell him thing, over and over again, that alone tells you that I still love and appreciate his support and his opinions. So he'll just have to get over the bad parts of this book and admit that it was all a part of my story, just like things I did that *I* would like to take out of the book. But if I'm trying to be *real* and *honest* about it, then I *can't* take those things out.

It is what it is—*Dior; Strip Club Diaries #1*. I had to find the courage to do it. But now I need to decide whose story I want to tell next. Who will tell the *Strip Club Diaries #2...*? I guess you'll all find out in a few of months after this one.

But now you know what the strip club life is all about—a bunch of girls who live, breathe, eat, sleep, drink, love, hate, cry, struggle, succeed and fail just like everybody else. We just happen to dance in sexy clothes for guys and girls who decide to pay us for it.

That's the American way. You do whatever you need to do to make your money. And I don't judge *anybody* for it—at least not anymore. You have to understand the *world* that they come first. And you have to understand their story before you try to judge them. *Then* you can say something about it. But until then... you don't really know these people like you *think* you do. So keep your comments to yourself until you know.